WOOPSII Journal
for Personal Accountability

•

Tasha Danvers

Tasha Danvers
10586 W Pico Blvd, Suite 215
Los Angeles CA, 90064
Email: woopsiijournal@gmail.com
tashadanvers.com

ISBN: 978-1-906869-17-5
Published by 77 Publishers
Cover Design by Tasha Danvers

CONTENT

I

Other Titles by Tasha Danvers

101 Motivational Card Deck

God's Promises NKJV Card Deck

You Got This! NKJV Card Deck

365 Scriptural Affirmations

Tazzo And The Extravaganza (children's book)
- percentage of proceeds to charity

Tazzo And The Stars (children's book)
- percentage of proceeds to charity

NOTE TO THE READER

Throughout this book I use the word God and prayer to reference a power and method of communication, that I believe in. It grounds me to be aware of a power higher than myself. If that doesn't work for you, replace it with whatever word or concept aligns with your understanding. Ultimately, the focus here is on the principles, so adapt as needed to resonate with your perspective.

Additionally, if you follow the Word of God, each day I encourage you to recite the Daily Decree & Declaration located at the back of your WOOPSII Journal.

DEDICATION

This book is dedicated to those of you who believed in me even when I didn't believe in myself. To those of you who have been patient and diligently prayerful in the foreground and the background, eager to see me one day get my *ish* together. This book is for those of you who see my light and never stop encouraging me to let it shine.
Most importantly, this book is intended for individuals similar to myself, who have faced challenges in

- maintaining consistency
- getting clarity on your goals, and
- who have '**should**' on themselves because you think that you haven't sufficiently accomplished what you "should" have by now.

Enough with the self-imposed "should-ing" on yourself; you're here for a reason, and it's no coincidence. This is your moment, and together, we'll strive purposefully for victory. Together we will Win On Purpose.

PS Mum, you're the love of my life. Not ever have you ever not been by my side or in the stands cheering me on, whether those were sports stands or life stands. Thank you forever! xoxo

PPS Jaden Wayde Smith, I will keep all the promises I made to you. <3

Habakkuk 2:2-3
2 Then the Lord answered me and said:
"Write the vision
And make it plain on tablets,
That he may run who reads it.
3 For the vision is yet for an appointed time;
But at the end it will speak, and it will not lie.
Though it tarries, wait for it;
Because it will surely come,
It will not tarry.

Why Accountability?

In England, the country where I was born, the phrase 'whoopsie-daisy' (informal) is used as a light- hearted way of acknowledging a mistake. For example, if a toddler falls over, you will often hear a parent lovingly say 'whoopsie-daisy'.

My use of the phrase WOOPSII here, is a play on words of sorts. Where 'whoopsie-daisy' is a mistake, WOOPSII is the complete opposite. WOOPSII is intentional, thought-out and purposeful. WOOPSII is an acronym that lays out a framework for your day with; Will, Outcome, Obstacles, Plan & Pray, See, Intention, and Invoice. I'll explain them all in more detail later.

As we strive each day to become better versions of ourselves, WOOPSII invites us to take a closer look, hold ourselves high, and be committed, intentional, and accountable for what we are creating in our lives.

That said, your WOOPSII JOURNAL is not just something to check off of your daily To Do list, it is a living, breathing part of creating your future outcomes.

I highly recommend that you use this journal with an accountability partner, or as part of an accountability group. Why!? I'm so glad you asked! As an Olympic medalist I can assure you that accountability played a huge role in my ability to stand on the Olympic podium in 2008. Full transparency, this was something I didn't realize until after I had retired, but I'll save that story for another book. What I will do though, is give you the cold hard facts on accountability, because you deserve that.

According to a study done by the American Society of Training and Development* (ASTD), we have a 65% chance of reaching a goal if we have an accountability partner. Amazing right!? Well, pick your jaw up because there's more. What ASTD also found in that study, was that our chances of successfully reaching a goal, rise to 95% when we establish an ongoing appointment with our accountability partners! Ah hello, what are you waiting for? Buy a copy of this journal for your serious goal-getting buddy and let's go!

Indeed, accountability is essential for those genuinely seeking results. By fully embracing it, you'll reap significant rewards and find yourself achieving success beyond measure. Your presence here is purposeful, not coincidental. Let's unite our efforts to deliberately and intentionally manifest the outcomes we truly desire.

We'll talk more about how to select the right accountability partner and what an accountability appointment should look like later. Then, if you feel you don't have the appropriate partner or group to take you to the next level in your life, simply reach out to us and we will support you in that mission.

In the meantime, let's get completely clear about what accountability is, and what it is not.

*ASTD Handbook of Measuring and Evaluating Training
By Patricia Pulliam Phillips, American Society for Training and Development
(available on Google Books)

What Exactly Is Accountability?

Here's the crux of the matter: accountability boils down to ***being responsible for your actions***. An Accountability Partner is the one who holds you to that responsibility. If you're serious about achieving your desired results, it's crucial to select a partner or group capable of fulfilling that role effectively. Let's delve into the details.

Tips on choosing an Accountability Partner:

- Whenever possible, seek out individuals who **share similar goals or interests**, or possess experience navigating the path you aim to travel, such as a coach or mentor. This ensures that both of you are working towards common objectives.

- Choose someone **reliable** that will be committed to supporting you and holding your feet to the fire.

- Seek someone that has a **communication style** that will support you in succeeding.

- For a more effective relationship, work with someone you **trust** and who trusts you.

- Someone with a **positive attitude** can go leaps and bounds to keeping you motivated, and helping you stay focused on your goals.

- Ensure that both you and your accountability partner have a similar level of **commitment** to the goals you're working towards. Mismatched commitment levels may lead to frustration.

Approach the selection of your Accountability Partner with care. Avoid simply choosing your grandma because she bakes cookies for you and will always let you off the hook!

(If you need support finding an accountability partner/group contact us at **woopsiijournal@gmail.com**)

Structuring your accountability.

Now that you've secured an exceptional Accountability Partner, it's time to deliberate and establish the frequency of your check-ins. My suggestion is to schedule meetings at least once a week, although some individuals opt for daily check-ins. Select a timetable that suits both parties' needs and availability.

Tips on structuring an Accountability Appointment:

Ok let me say this loud and clear... An accountability appointment isn't an opportunity for casual conversation about workplace annoyances or dinner choices. It's a concentrated session aimed at keeping you on course and advancing toward your goals. Here are some tips for effectively managing your sessions.

- Punctuality is key. Respect the time of others by being on time. No one wants to wait around and listen to excuses for tardiness.

- With a one-to-one, keep appointments to 15 minutes or less (use good judgement for larger groups).

Do your best to stick to this Accountability Success Framework ASF:

- What relevant WINS/PROGRESS did you make toward your goals.
  - For the sake of this process I recommend focusing on no more than 3 major goals at a time. Have one that is your **Hot Ticket Goal**. That is the one goal that if you achieve it, everything else will be easier or unnecessary.
  - Discuss the wins you had this week, primarily in relation to your **HTG**.

- What were your SETBACKS/CHALLENGES?
  - What if anything, held you up, set you back, or became challenging? This could be a situation, a person, etc.

- What CORRECTIONS/FIXES need to be made to overcome that?
  - Brainstorm what can be done to overcome this challenge and what are the possible fixes, then make a plan to implement them.

- Is SUPPORT NEEDED and if so who could support you?
  - I have met so many people, present company included, that hinder their success because they are uncomfortable, afraid, too proud, too shy (insert your excuse here), to ask for the help or support they really need. Time's a-ticking, don't let that be you. Get clear on what support you need and who or what can provide that.

- What was your KEY LEARNING point this week?
  - What is at least one thing you learned this week? It could be something about yourself, a process, a system, people around you, your business, etc

- What are your ACTION STEPS for the coming week and your BY WHEN to complete each step?
  - A key step in success is knowing what you are going to get up to in the coming days. What are the action steps you will complete during the week and by when will you complete them. Don't just say by next week, have a clear idea of the exact day (and time where possible), when you will be able to complete it. If you are unsure, simply give it your best guess based on the information you currently have.

Accountability Success Framework

At the back of this journal you will find ASF pages like the one below with an example of how to complete it.

DATE:

Accountability Success Framework

Accountability Partner

Accountability Partner's (HTG) Hot Ticket Goal

WINS /PROGRESS

SETBACKS / CHALLENGES

CORRECTIONS / FIXES

SUPPORT NEEDED

KEY LEARNING

ACTION STEPS & BY WHEN

Why Is Having An Accountability Partner So Effective?

After reviewing those ASTD statistics on accountability, you might be asking yourself, "What makes it so much more effective than going solo? I'm self motivated!" Well, having an accountability partner can provide numerous advantages, as they are dedicated to playing a vital role in fostering your personal and professional development. To help you grasp the significance of an Accountability Partner, here are some key benefits of this partnership:

1. **Increased Motivation:** Knowing that someone else is aware of your goals and progress can boost your motivation. The desire to meet expectations and not let your partner down can drive you to stay focused and work harder.

2. **Consistent Progress:** Regular check-ins with your accountability partner create a structure for progress tracking. This consistency helps you stay on track and ensures that you make continuous efforts toward your goals.

3. **Objective Perspective:** An accountability partner can offer an objective viewpoint on your challenges and achievements. They provide constructive feedback and insights, helping you overcome obstacles and make informed decisions.

4. **Shared Resources and Ideas:** Collaborating with someone who shares similar goals can lead to the exchange of valuable resources, ideas, and strategies. This sharing of knowledge can enhance your approach and broaden your perspective.

5. **Increased Accountability:** The act of sharing your goals with someone else makes you more accountable for your actions. The sense of responsibility to your partner can prevent

procrastination and encourage timely goal completion.

6. **Emotional Support:** Pursuing goals can be challenging, and having someone to share both successes and setbacks with can provide emotional support. Your accountability partner can offer encouragement during tough times and celebrate achievements with you.

7. **Greater Commitment:** When you commit to someone else, the level of commitment often increases. This commitment extends beyond personal accountability, reinforcing your dedication to the goals you've set.

8. **Building a Sense of Community:** Working with an accountability partner creates a sense of community and shared purpose. Knowing that you are not alone in your journey fosters a supportive environment that can be motivating and uplifting.

9. **Enhanced Problem-Solving:** Two heads are often better than one. Your accountability partner can contribute different perspectives and solutions to challenges you may face, aiding in more effective problem-solving.

10. **Strengthened Relationships:** Collaborating on goals with someone else can strengthen your relationship with your accountability partner. The shared experience of growth and achievement can create a bond that extends beyond your individual pursuits.

Basically, an accountability partner provides a combination of motivation, support, and shared resources that can significantly contribute to your success in achieving personal and professional goals.

Getting Started

1. Select a 90-Day Hot Ticket Goal (**HTG**), along with up to two additional goals that will be your main focus.
2. Find an Accountability Partner (**AP**) or group.
3. Set a regular appointment time with your group or partner (preferably the same time and day each week).
4. During your sessions, ensure you ask pertinent questions and manage your time effectively. Utilize the Accountability Success Framework (**ASF**) provided in this journal. If additional time is required for brainstorming or other tasks, schedule a separate meeting accordingly.
5. Be honest in your communication and truly hold each other accountable.
6. Stay committed to accountability. Regularly assess progress together to ensure the partnership is effective. Even if you have a strong rapport with your partner, it's acceptable to seek a new partner if the current arrangement isn't conducive to achieving the specific goal. However, be mindful to differentiate between the need for a new partner and deeper issues like avoidance or procrastination.

Next Steps

- Write your 90-Day goals in the spaces provided in this journal.
- Each morning complete the day section of your journal.
- Each evening complete the night section of your journal.
- At least once a week, with your Accountability Partner, go through the **ASF** section of your journal.
- Each day, as an added measure of accountability, I encourage you to consider sharing a photo of a portion or all of your daily WOOPSII entry with your **AP** (optional)

The WOOPSII Process

MORNING SESSION

WILL

Consider this your declaration of intent for the day - what you're committed to accomplishing. What you WILL do. If you're stretching yourself it will most likely also require *will* (determination) on your part.

OUTCOME

The power of energy and vibration is undeniable, influencing our thoughts, actions, and feelings, and ultimately impacting our ability to achieve desired outcomes. It's crucial for us to gain clarity on our desired emotional state because feelings are often the driving force behind our actions and thus our results. We don't pursue objectives merely for their tangible aspects; rather, we seek them for the emotions they evoke—whether it's pride, security, fulfillment, peace of mind, or any other sentiment. So here we define what emotions we aspire to experience once we accomplish our daily intentions.

OBSTACLES

Being proactive in identifying potential obstacles that could hinder your daily goal achievement is an effective strategy for prevention or resolution. This is where we will also be able to clarify whether these obstacles stem from internal or external sources.

PLAN & PRAY

Now that you've established your daily goals, identified

the desired emotions associated with those achievements, and recognized potential obstacles, it's time to devise a plan to ensure success. For instance, outline specific timeframes for completing tasks and commit to minimizing distractions by turning off your phone to avoid interruptions from social media or calls.
As Benjamin Franklin wisely said, "If you fail to plan, you are planning to fail!"
Additionally, this is an opportune moment to pause, pray, and declare that your desired outcomes are already manifest, with the support of a higher power guiding you in executing your daily vision.

SEE
The subconscious mind operates through images. 90 to 95% of our daily thoughts, actions, and behaviors are governed by the subconscious mind and subconscious programming. Breaking habits can be challenging for many individuals, as their conscious will, may not align with their subconscious programming, the part of the mind which actually dictates their behavior.

However, the concept of neuroplasticity offers hope. Neuroplasticity refers to our brain's ability to reprogram and rewire itself. By repeatedly delivering certain behaviors and images to our subconscious minds, we create an environment conducive to transformation, renewal, and reprogramming.

Visualization and imagination play pivotal roles in

creating a new vision for our lives by reprogramming the subconscious. Imagining involves creating a mental picture of something already experienced, whereas visualization taps into senses to envision something yet to be experienced. For instance, a person can imagine eating chocolate ice cream because they've done it before, but visualizing speaking in front of a stadium filled with 500,000 people requires visualizing an unfamiliar scenario if never experienced before.

It's crucial not to overlook this step. Utilize the clarity gained from previous steps to elevate your visualization. With a clear understanding of how you want to feel, visualize yourself experiencing the exact day you desire. I recommend dedicating at least 60 seconds for daily events, and an average of 15 minutes, to visualization of life goals for optimal results.

INTENTION

Consider this as an affirmation of who you're choosing to embody today – perhaps poised, aware, or wise. Abraham Hicks, in "Ask and It Is Given," often discusses Segment Intending, which involves setting intentions for specific segments of time, whether it's a day, week, month, or year. It's advisable to practice this as may times as possible throughout your day.

For instance, as you observe the school bus arriving outside, you might declare, "My intention is to be fully present with my children as they share their school day experiences."

INVOICE

I was profoundly inspired when my mentor and business partner, Yvonne Brooks, introduced me to this transformative concept. It involves acknowledging the value I offer to the Universe, to God, for my time, services, products, talents, and more.

In this section, you reflect on the actions you've taken or will take throughout the day without any sense of guilt in regards to it's monetary value. For instance, if you provide care for a parent without financial compensation, yet you believe the impact of your contribution is equivalent to $5,000 per hour, you can invoice the Spirit for that value. Even if you do receive compensation, it's okay to acknowledge you It's remarkable how this simple action can lead to astonishing results in what you attract into your life.

POWER QUESTION

Yvonne Brooks significantly emphasized the importance and potency of questions for me. Did you know that there are over 3,000 questions in the Bible? Precisely 3,294, as stated by www.openthebible.org. Have you ever observed how Jesus often responded to questions with questions himself? It's intriguing, isn't it? But why does he do that? Because questions hold immense power.

One particular insight from Yvonne resonated deeply with me: "You live the answer to your questions. So what questions are you asking?" It's like a mic drop moment! Your life's circumstances often reflect the questions you're asking, or sometimes, not asking at all.

This is a critical aspect that should not be underestimated. There are questions that resonate with low vibrations, disempowering us, and then there are those that elevate our spirits, empowering us.

For instance, when faced with a challenge, a low vibration question might be "Why me!?" On the other hand, a high vibration question could be "How can I become someone who handles challenges with poise, confidence, and grace?"

Each day, take this opportunity to craft the most empowering question relevant to your goals. When pondering the question, consider whether the answer aligns with experiences you wish to manifest. Would you rather live the answer to "Why can't I ever get anything right?" or to "How can I attract and recognize all the Destiny Angels in my life here to support my vision and growth?" I believe I can anticipate your preference. wink wink

VISION

Now that we've emphasized the significance of visualization and imagination, let's reaffirm that truth by incorporating it into this section. Here, you'll sketch an image representing your daily goal. I understand not everyone has artistic prowess, but I'm not expecting a masterpiece. Even a simple stick figure will suffice. However, the depiction should be images or a combination of images and words, not solely words.

GRATITUDE

"Be thankful for what you have and you'll end up having more. If you concentrate on what you don't have, you will never, ever have enough." - Oprah

"Your gratitude is magnetic, and the more gratitude you have, the more abundance you magnetize. It is Universal law!" — Rhonda Byrne, The Magic

You heard the ladies! So let's get some gratitude going on up in here! Now, I get it, it can be tough sometimes, especially when your mind is questioning, "How can I feel grateful for this bill I can't afford to pay?" But trust me, from personal experience, there's always something to be grateful for. If you're still breathing, things could always be worse. Become a Gratitude Seeker. Make it a daily practice to reflect on all the things you have to be thankful for. Remember, gratitude has the power to transform your life. Embrace it!

JOURNAL

This section has no restrictions. It's a blank canvas for you to jot down whatever comes to mind—your thoughts, ideas, or reflections. You might choose to summarize your day, outline your plans for tomorrow, or celebrate achievements from the day. Your journal is entirely yours to fill as you please. After journaling, rate your effectiveness. If your score falls below 10, consider ways to enhance your effectiveness tomorrow or in the upcoming days.

Let's Begin!

rite your goals in the spaces provided.

MY HOT TICKET GOAL

GOAL 2

GOAL 3

YOUR WHY

Your WHY is so important that Simon Sinek wrote an entire book about it called Start With Why. So in this section we'll take his advice and start with WHY.

You really want to go as deep as you can with this question, because this is the part of your process that will allow you to get through the difficult times (which I can pretty much guarantee will come at some point).

Don't settle with the first answer that comes to mind. Ask yourself 'Why is that important to me?' Then when you give yourself that answer, ask yourself Why is that important to me?' Then, when you give yourself that answer, ask yourself 'Why is that important to me?' No that wasn't a typo.

Some personal development gurus say that you should ask yourself why a goal is important to you at least 7 times before you'll actually get close to the real answer. It's called the Seven Levels of Why and I would encourage you to do it.

When you've gotten to the deepest level, write your answer in the space provided on the next page. Just do your best to go beyond the surface, don't beat yourself up if you don't get to 7 levels.

EXAMPLE

7 Levels of WHY

1. I want to buy my own home and that's important to
2. Because I want to feel like I own something of value and that's important to m
3. Because I never had anything of value growing up and that's important to m
4. Because I dont want Riley to have the same experience and that's important to me...
5. Because I want to break the legacy of going without and that's important to me...
6. Because I have seen too many people in my family suffering. and that's important to me...
7. Because I know it's time to end the legacy of suffering. and that's important to me

Line #7 - My WHY - I want to buy my own home as a step in breaking the legacy suffering in my family

MY WHY - HTG

MY WHY - GOAL 2

MY WHY - GOAL 3

DATE:

Write in complete sentences. i.e "Today I am...", "When I accomplish this..."

WILL

Declaration of intent for the day. What you will do.

Today I am finishing my business plan, getting back in the weight room, and taking some self care time for at least 30 minutes.

OUTCOME

What you will feel when you accomplish this?

I will feel a sense of peace and pride that I am sticking to my commitments.

OBSTACLES

What could get in the way of you getting these things done?

Working too late and being too tired for the gym. Getting distracted.

PLAN & PRAY

What is the plan/how will you make sure it gets done? Then pray on it.

I will stick to my schedule and not let distractions throw me off course. I will workout in the morning, take a nap and then start my business plan.

SEE

Imagine your day getting it all done and how it feels (60 seconds)

INTENSION

Who I want to BE today – e.g poised, aware, wise

Today I am focused, confident, calm, and determined.

INVOICE

Do you need to invoice the spirit for anything?

Coaching session with Juliana $7,500 for 90 minute session.

"Wisdom is the reward you get for a lifetime of listening when you'd have preferred to talk." --Doug Larson

DATE:

POWER QUESTION

Who do I need to become to create a business that makes $500K/year? How do I become an impactful business owner?

VISION

Every day in every way I'm getting better, better and better! I am blessed and highly favored.

GRATITUDE

I am grateful for the support of my family, and community, and the ability to get up and go to the gym with no health issues.

JOURNAL

Today was a great day! I actually manifested the business connection I put on my WOOPS!! last week! We're meeting tomorrow for an initial discussion on how we might move forward and I'm so excited. Workout went great too and you'll be glad to know I finished my 1st draft of my business plan. Tomorrow, I'm going to ask my accountability partner if she'll take a look at it.

(1 = not effective, 10 = extremely effective)

On a scale of 1 - 10, How would you rate your effectiveness today? 1 2 3 4 5 6 7 8 (9) 10

Definitely need to turn the TV off in the background when I'm working

DATE:

Write in complete sentences. i.e "Today I am...", "When I accomplish this..."

WILL

Declaration of intent for the day. What you will do.

OUTCOME

What you will feel when you accomplish this?

OBSTACLES

What could get in the way of you getting these things done?

PLAN & PRAY

What is the plan/how will you make sure it gets done? Then pray on it.

SEE

Imagine your day getting it all done and how it feels (60 seconds)

INTENSION

Who I want to BE today – e.g poised, aware, wise

INVOICE

Do you need to invoice the spirit for anything?

"Wisdom is the reward you get for a lifetime of listening when you'd have preferred to talk." --Doug Larson

DATE:

POWER QUESTION

VISION

Every day in every way I'm getting better, better and better! I am blessed and highly favored.

GRATITUDE

JOURNAL

On a scale of 1 - 10, How would you rate your effectiveness today? 1 2 3 4 5 6 7 8 9 10

DATE:

Write in complete sentences. i.e "Today I am...", "When I accomplish this..."

WILL

Declaration of intent for the day. What you will do.

OUTCOME

What you will feel when you accomplish this?

OBSTACLES

What could get in the way of you getting these things done?

PLAN & PRAY

What is the plan/how will you make sure it gets done? Then pray on it.

SEE

Imagine your day getting it all done and how it feels (60 seconds)

INTENSION

Who I want to BE today – e.g poised, aware, wise

INVOICE

Do you need to invoice the spirit for anything?

Every human being is the author of his/her own health or disease
Budda

ATE:

POWER QUESTION

VISION

Every day in every way I'm getting better, better and better! I am blessed and highly favored.

GRATITUDE

JOURNAL

On a scale of 1 - 10, How would you rate your effectiveness today? 1 2 3 4 5 6 7 8 9 10

DATE:

Write in complete sentences. i.e "Today I am...", "When I accomplish this..."

WILL

Declaration of intent for the day. What you will do.

OUTCOME

What you will feel when you accomplish this?

OBSTACLES

What could get in the way of you getting these things done?

PLAN & PRAY

What is the plan/how will you make sure it gets done? Then pray on it.

SEE

Imagine your day getting it all done and how it feels (60 seconds)

INTENSION

Who I want to BE today – e.g poised, aware, wise

INVOICE

Do you need to invoice the spirit for anything?

"Health is the greatest gift, contentment the greatest wealth, faithfulness the best relationship." - Buddha

DATE:

POWER QUESTION

VISION

Every day in every way I'm getting better, better and better! I am blessed and highly favored.

GRATITUDE

JOURNAL

On a scale of 1 - 10, How would you rate your effectiveness today? 1 2 3 4 5 6 7 8 9 10

DATE:

Write in complete sentences. i.e "Today I am...", "When I accomplish this..."

WILL

Declaration of intent for the day. What you will do.

OUTCOME

What you will feel when you accomplish this?

OBSTACLES

What could get in the way of you getting these things done?

PLAN & PRAY

What is the plan/how will you make sure it gets done? Then pray on it.

SEE

Imagine your day getting it all done and how it feels (60 seconds)

INTENSION

Who I want to BE today – e.g poised, aware, wise

INVOICE

Do you need to invoice the spirit for anything?

"One of the most sincere forms of respect is actually listening to what another has to say."
--Bryant H. McGill

DATE:

POWER QUESTION

VISION

Every day in every way I'm getting better, better and better! I am blessed and highly favored.

GRATITUDE

JOURNAL

On a scale of 1 - 10, How would you rate your effectiveness today? 1 2 3 4 5 6 7 8 9 10

DATE:

Write in complete sentences. i.e "Today I am...", "When I accomplish this..."

WILL

Declaration of intent for the day. What you will do.

OUTCOME

What you will feel when you accomplish this?

OBSTACLES

What could get in the way of you getting these things done?

PLAN & PRAY

What is the plan/how will you make sure it gets done? Then pray on it.

SEE

Imagine your day getting it all done and how it feels (60 seconds)

INTENSION

Who I want to BE today – e.g poised, aware, wise

INVOICE

Do you need to invoice the spirit for anything?

"Life is far too important a thing ever to talk seriously about." -Oscar Wilde

DATE:

POWER QUESTION

VISION

Every day in every way I'm getting better, better and better! I am blessed and highly favored.

GRATITUDE

JOURNAL

On a scale of 1 - 10, How would you rate your effectiveness today? 1 2 3 4 5 6 7 8 9 10

DATE:

Write in complete sentences. i.e "Today I am...", "When I accomplish this..."

WILL

Declaration of intent for the day. What you will do.

OUTCOME

What you will feel when you accomplish this?

OBSTACLES

What could get in the way of you getting these things done?

PLAN & PRAY

What is the plan/how will you make sure it gets done? Then pray on it.

SEE

Imagine your day getting it all done and how it feels (60 seconds)

INTENSION

Who I want to BE today – e.g poised, aware, wise

INVOICE

Do you need to invoice the spirit for anything?

"I go to nature to be soothed and healed, and to have my senses put in order." - John Burroughs

DATE:

POWER QUESTION

VISION

Every day in every way I'm getting better, better and better! I am blessed and highly favored.

GRATITUDE

JOURNAL

On a scale of 1 - 10, How would you rate your effectiveness today? 1 2 3 4 5 6 7 8 9 10

DATE:

Write in complete sentences. i.e "Today I am...", "When I accomplish this..."

WILL

Declaration of intent for the day. What you will do.

OUTCOME

What you will feel when you accomplish this?

OBSTACLES

What could get in the way of you getting these things done?

PLAN & PRAY

What is the plan/how will you make sure it gets done? Then pray on it.

SEE

Imagine your day getting it all done and how it feels (60 seconds)

INTENSION

Who I want to BE today – e.g poised, aware, wise

INVOICE

Do you need to invoice the spirit for anything?

"Kindness is a language which the deaf can hear and the blind can see." -Mark Twain

DATE:

POWER QUESTION

VISION

Every day in every way I'm getting better, better and better! I am blessed and highly favored.

GRATITUDE

JOURNAL

On a scale of 1 - 10, How would you rate your effectiveness today? 1 2 3 4 5 6 7 8 9 10

DATE:

Write in complete sentences. i.e "Today I am...", "When I accomplish this..."

WILL

Declaration of intent for the day. What you will do.

OUTCOME

What you will feel when you accomplish this?

OBSTACLES

What could get in the way of you getting these things done?

PLAN & PRAY

What is the plan/how will you make sure it gets done? Then pray on it.

SEE

Imagine your day getting it all done and how it feels (60 seconds)

INTENSION

Who I want to BE today – e.g poised, aware, wise

INVOICE

Do you need to invoice the spirit for anything?

"The greatest use of life is to spend it for something that will outlast it." -- William James

DATE:

POWER QUESTION

VISION

Every day in every way I'm getting better, better and better! I am blessed and highly favored.

GRATITUDE

JOURNAL

On a scale of 1 - 10, How would you rate your effectiveness today? 1 2 3 4 5 6 7 8 9 10

DATE:

Write in complete sentences. i.e "Today I am...", "When I accomplish this..."

WILL

Declaration of intent for the day. What you will do.

OUTCOME

What you will feel when you accomplish this?

OBSTACLES

What could get in the way of you getting these things done?

PLAN & PRAY

What is the plan/how will you make sure it gets done? Then pray on it.

SEE

Imagine your day getting it all done and how it feels (60 seconds)

INTENSION

Who I want to BE today – e.g poised, aware, wise

INVOICE

Do you need to invoice the spirit for anything?

"I think that if you keep your eyes and your ears open and you are receptive to learning, there are skills you can get from any job at all."--Cat Deeley

DATE:

POWER QUESTION

VISION

Every day in every way I'm getting better, better and better! I am blessed and highly favored.

GRATITUDE

JOURNAL

On a scale of 1 - 10, How would you rate your effectiveness today? 1 2 3 4 5 6 7 8 9 10

DATE:

Write in complete sentences. i.e "Today I am...", "When I accomplish this..."

WILL

Declaration of intent for the day. What you will do.

OUTCOME

What you will feel when you accomplish this?

OBSTACLES

What could get in the way of you getting these things done?

PLAN & PRAY

What is the plan/how will you make sure it gets done? Then pray on it.

SEE

Imagine your day getting it all done and how it feels (60 seconds)

INTENSION

Who I want to BE today – e.g poised, aware, wise

INVOICE

Do you need to invoice the spirit for anything?

"He who has health has hope; and he who has hope, has everything." - Thomas Carlyle

DATE:

POWER QUESTION

VISION

Every day in every way I'm getting better, better and better! I am blessed and highly favored.

GRATITUDE

JOURNAL

On a scale of 1 - 10, How would you rate your effectiveness today? 1 2 3 4 5 6 7 8 9 10

DATE:

Write in complete sentences. i.e "Today I am...", "When I accomplish this..."

WILL

Declaration of intent for the day. What you will do.

OUTCOME

What you will feel when you accomplish this?

OBSTACLES

What could get in the way of you getting these things done?

PLAN & PRAY

What is the plan/how will you make sure it gets done? Then pray on it.

SEE

Imagine your day getting it all done and how it feels (60 seconds)

INTENSION

Who I want to BE today – e.g poised, aware, wise

INVOICE

Do you need to invoice the spirit for anything?

"Anger can have equally disastrous effects on your own life. Left unchecked, it can destroy some of your closest relationships and undermine your physical and mental health." - Albert Ellis

DATE:

POWER QUESTION

VISION

Every day in every way I'm getting better, better and better! I am blessed and highly favored.

GRATITUDE

JOURNAL

On a scale of 1 - 10, How would you rate your effectiveness today? 1 2 3 4 5 6 7 8 9 10

DATE:

Write in complete sentences. i.e "Today I am...", "When I accomplish this..."

WILL

Declaration of intent for the day. What you will do.

OUTCOME

What you will feel when you accomplish this?

OBSTACLES

What could get in the way of you getting these things done?

PLAN & PRAY

What is the plan/how will you make sure it gets done? Then pray on it.

SEE

Imagine your day getting it all done and how it feels (60 seconds)

INTENSION

Who I want to BE today – e.g poised, aware, wise

INVOICE

Do you need to invoice the spirit for anything?

"I have chosen to be happy because it is good for my health." - Voltaire

DATE:

POWER QUESTION

VISION

Every day in every way I'm getting better, better and better! I am blessed and highly favored.

GRATITUDE

JOURNAL

On a scale of 1 - 10, How would you rate your effectiveness today? 1 2 3 4 5 6 7 8 9 10

DATE:

Write in complete sentences. i.e "Today I am...", "When I accomplish this..."

WILL

Declaration of intent for the day. What you will do.

OUTCOME

What you will feel when you accomplish this?

OBSTACLES

What could get in the way of you getting these things done?

PLAN & PRAY

What is the plan/how will you make sure it gets done? Then pray on it.

SEE

Imagine your day getting it all done and how it feels (60 seconds)

INTENSION

Who I want to BE today – e.g poised, aware, wise

INVOICE

Do you need to invoice the spirit for anything?

"There is overwhelming evidence that the higher the level of self-esteem, the more likely one will be to treat others with respect, kindness, and generosity." -Nathaniel Branden

DATE:

POWER QUESTION

VISION

Every day in every way I'm getting better, better and better! I am blessed and highly favored.

GRATITUDE

JOURNAL

On a scale of 1 - 10, How would you rate your effectiveness today? 1 2 3 4 5 6 7 8 9 10

DATE:

Write in complete sentences. i.e "Today I am...", "When I accomplish this..."

WILL

Declaration of intent for the day. What you will do.

OUTCOME

What you will feel when you accomplish this?

OBSTACLES

What could get in the way of you getting these things done?

PLAN & PRAY

What is the plan/how will you make sure it gets done? Then pray on it.

SEE

Imagine your day getting it all done and how it feels (60 seconds)

INTENSION

Who I want to BE today – e.g poised, aware, wise

INVOICE

Do you need to invoice the spirit for anything?

"Sometimes reality is too complex. Stories give it form." --Jean Luc Godard

DATE:

POWER QUESTION

VISION

Every day in every way I'm getting better, better and better! I am blessed and highly favored.

GRATITUDE

JOURNAL

On a scale of 1 - 10, How would you rate your effectiveness today? 1 2 3 4 5 6 7 8 9 10

DATE:

Write in complete sentences. i.e "Today I am...", "When I accomplish this..."

WILL

Declaration of intent for the day. What you will do.

OUTCOME

What you will feel when you accomplish this?

OBSTACLES

What could get in the way of you getting these things done?

PLAN & PRAY

What is the plan/how will you make sure it gets done? Then pray on it.

SEE

Imagine your day getting it all done and how it feels (60 seconds)

INTENSION

Who I want to BE today – e.g poised, aware, wise

INVOICE

Do you need to invoice the spirit for anything?

"If you succumb to the temptation of using violence in the struggle, unborn generations will be the recipients of a long and desolate night of bitterness, and your chief legacy to the future will be an endless reign of meaningless chaos." --Martin Luther King, Jr.

DATE:

POWER QUESTION

VISION

Every day in every way I'm getting better, better and better! I am blessed and highly favored.

GRATITUDE

JOURNAL

On a scale of 1 - 10, How would you rate your effectiveness today? 1 2 3 4 5 6 7 8 9 10

DATE:

Write in complete sentences. i.e "Today I am...", "When I accomplish this..."

WILL

Declaration of intent for the day. What you will do.

OUTCOME

What you will feel when you accomplish this?

OBSTACLES

What could get in the way of you getting these things done?

PLAN & PRAY

What is the plan/how will you make sure it gets done? Then pray on it.

SEE

Imagine your day getting it all done and how it feels (60 seconds)

INTENSION

Who I want to BE today – e.g poised, aware, wise

INVOICE

Do you need to invoice the spirit for anything?

No matter how much it gets abused, the body can restore balance. The first rule is to stop interfering with nature." - Deepak Chopra

DATE:

POWER QUESTION

VISION

Every day in every way I'm getting better, better and better! I am blessed and highly favored.

GRATITUDE

JOURNAL

On a scale of 1 - 10, How would you rate your effectiveness today? 1 2 3 4 5 6 7 8 9 10

DATE:

Write in complete sentences. i.e "Today I am...", "When I accomplish this..."

WILL

Declaration of intent for the day. What you will do.

OUTCOME

What you will feel when you accomplish this?

OBSTACLES

What could get in the way of you getting these things done?

PLAN & PRAY

What is the plan/how will you make sure it gets done? Then pray on it.

SEE

Imagine your day getting it all done and how it feels (60 seconds)

INTENSION

Who I want to BE today – e.g poised, aware, wise

INVOICE

Do you need to invoice the spirit for anything?

"If you have an important point to make, don't try to be subtle or clever. Use a pile driver. Hit the point once. Then come back and hit it again. Then hit it a third time--a tremendous whack." - Winston Churchill

DATE:

POWER QUESTION

VISION

Every day in every way I'm getting better, better and better! I am blessed and highly favored.

GRATITUDE

JOURNAL

On a scale of 1 - 10, How would you rate your effectiveness today? 1 2 3 4 5 6 7 8 9 10

DATE:

Write in complete sentences. i.e "Today I am...", "When I accomplish this..."

WILL

Declaration of intent for the day. What you will do.

OUTCOME

What you will feel when you accomplish this?

OBSTACLES

What could get in the way of you getting these things done?

PLAN & PRAY

What is the plan/how will you make sure it gets done? Then pray on it.

SEE

Imagine your day getting it all done and how it feels (60 seconds)

INTENSION

Who I want to BE today – e.g poised, aware, wise

INVOICE

Do you need to invoice the spirit for anything?

"You can't control what goes on outside, but you CAN control what goes on inside." - Unknown

ATE:

POWER QUESTION

VISION

Every day in every way I'm getting better, better and better! I am blessed and highly favored.

GRATITUDE

JOURNAL

On a scale of 1 - 10, How would you rate your effectiveness today? 1 2 3 4 5 6 7 8 9 10

DATE:

Write in complete sentences. i.e "Today I am...", "When I accomplish this..."

WILL

Declaration of intent for the day. What you will do.

OUTCOME

What you will feel when you accomplish this?

OBSTACLES

What could get in the way of you getting these things done?

PLAN & PRAY

What is the plan/how will you make sure it gets done? Then pray on it.

SEE

Imagine your day getting it all done and how it feels (60 seconds)

INTENSION

Who I want to BE today – e.g poised, aware, wise

INVOICE

Do you need to invoice the spirit for anything?

"Our kindness may be the most persuasive argument for that which we believe." -Gordon B. Hinckley

DATE:

POWER QUESTION

VISION

Every day in every way I'm getting better, better and better! I am blessed and highly favored.

GRATITUDE

JOURNAL

On a scale of 1 - 10, How would you rate your effectiveness today? 1 2 3 4 5 6 7 8 9 10

DATE:

Write in complete sentences. i.e "Today I am...", "When I accomplish this..."

WILL

Declaration of intent for the day. What you will do.

OUTCOME

What you will feel when you accomplish this?

OBSTACLES

What could get in the way of you getting these things done?

PLAN & PRAY

What is the plan/how will you make sure it gets done? Then pray on it.

SEE

Imagine your day getting it all done and how it feels (60 seconds)

INTENSION

Who I want to BE today – e.g poised, aware, wise

INVOICE

Do you need to invoice the spirit for anything?

"Have more humility. Remember you don't know the limits of your own abilities. Successful or not, if you keep pushing beyond yourself, you will enrich your own life--and maybe even please a few strangers." A.L. Kennedy

DATE:

POWER QUESTION

VISION

Every day in every way I'm getting better, better and better! I am blessed and highly favored.

GRATITUDE

JOURNAL

On a scale of 1 - 10, How would you rate your effectiveness today? 1 2 3 4 5 6 7 8 9 10

DATE:

Write in complete sentences. i.e "Today I am...", "When I accomplish this..."

WILL

Declaration of intent for the day. What you will do.

OUTCOME

What you will feel when you accomplish this?

OBSTACLES

What could get in the way of you getting these things done?

PLAN & PRAY

What is the plan/how will you make sure it gets done? Then pray on it.

SEE

Imagine your day getting it all done and how it feels (60 seconds)

INTENSION

Who I want to BE today – e.g poised, aware, wise

INVOICE

Do you need to invoice the spirit for anything?

"You can't leave a footprint that lasts if you're always walking on tiptoe." --Marion Blakely

DATE:

POWER QUESTION

VISION

Every day in every way I'm getting better, better and better! I am blessed and highly favored.

GRATITUDE

JOURNAL

On a scale of 1 - 10, How would you rate your effectiveness today? 1 2 3 4 5 6 7 8 9 10

DATE:

Write in complete sentences. i.e "Today I am...", "When I accomplish this..."

WILL

Declaration of intent for the day. What you will do.

OUTCOME

What you will feel when you accomplish this?

OBSTACLES

What could get in the way of you getting these things done?

PLAN & PRAY

What is the plan/how will you make sure it gets done? Then pray on it.

SEE

Imagine your day getting it all done and how it feels (60 seconds)

INTENSION

Who I want to BE today – e.g poised, aware, wise

INVOICE

Do you need to invoice the spirit for anything?

"Throughout history, great healers have discovered the power of breathing to enhance the physical, mental, and spiritual well-being of their people." - Richard P. Brown

DATE:

POWER QUESTION

VISION

Every day in every way I'm getting better, better and better! I am blessed and highly favored.

GRATITUDE

JOURNAL

On a scale of 1 - 10, How would you rate your effectiveness today? 1 2 3 4 5 6 7 8 9 10

DATE:

Write in complete sentences. i.e "Today I am...", "When I accomplish this..."

WILL

Declaration of intent for the day. What you will do.

OUTCOME

What you will feel when you accomplish this?

OBSTACLES

What could get in the way of you getting these things done?

PLAN & PRAY

What is the plan/how will you make sure it gets done? Then pray on it.

SEE

Imagine your day getting it all done and how it feels (60 seconds)

INTENSION

Who I want to BE today – e.g poised, aware, wise

INVOICE

Do you need to invoice the spirit for anything?

"A story to me means a plot where there is some surprise. Because that is how life is--full of surprises." -Isaac Bashevis Singer

DATE:

POWER QUESTION

VISION

Every day in every way I'm getting better, better and better! I am blessed and highly favored.

GRATITUDE

JOURNAL

On a scale of 1 - 10, How would you rate your effectiveness today? 1 2 3 4 5 6 7 8 9 10

DATE:

Write in complete sentences. i.e "Today I am...", "When I accomplish this..."

WILL

Declaration of intent for the day. What you will do.

OUTCOME

What you will feel when you accomplish this?

OBSTACLES

What could get in the way of you getting these things done?

PLAN & PRAY

What is the plan/how will you make sure it gets done? Then pray on it.

SEE

Imagine your day getting it all done and how it feels (60 seconds)

INTENSION

Who I want to BE today – e.g poised, aware, wise

INVOICE

Do you need to invoice the spirit for anything?

"Shine with all you have. When someone tries to blow you out, just take their oxygen and burn brighter." --Katelyn S. Irons

DATE:

POWER QUESTION

VISION

Every day in every way I'm getting better, better and better! I am blessed and highly favored.

GRATITUDE

JOURNAL

On a scale of 1 - 10, How would you rate your effectiveness today? 1 2 3 4 5 6 7 8 9 10

DATE:

Write in complete sentences. i.e "Today I am...", "When I accomplish this..."

WILL

Declaration of intent for the day. What you will do.

OUTCOME

What you will feel when you accomplish this?

OBSTACLES

What could get in the way of you getting these things done?

PLAN & PRAY

What is the plan/how will you make sure it gets done? Then pray on it.

SEE

Imagine your day getting it all done and how it feels (60 seconds)

INTENSION

Who I want to BE today – e.g poised, aware, wise

INVOICE

Do you need to invoice the spirit for anything?

"You can complain because roses have thorns, or you can be grateful that thorn bushes have roses." - Tom Wilson

DATE:

POWER QUESTION

VISION

Every day in every way I'm getting better, better and better! I am blessed and highly favored.

GRATITUDE

JOURNAL

On a scale of 1 - 10, How would you rate your effectiveness today? 1 2 3 4 5 6 7 8 9 10

DATE:

Write in complete sentences. i.e "Today I am...", "When I accomplish this..."

WILL

Declaration of intent for the day. What you will do.

OUTCOME

What you will feel when you accomplish this?

OBSTACLES

What could get in the way of you getting these things done?

PLAN & PRAY

What is the plan/how will you make sure it gets done? Then pray on it.

SEE

Imagine your day getting it all done and how it feels (60 seconds)

INTENSION

Who I want to BE today – e.g poised, aware, wise

INVOICE

Do you need to invoice the spirit for anything?

"Winners lose much more often than losers. So if you keep losing but you're still trying, keep it up! You're right on track."--Matthew Keith Groves

DATE:

POWER QUESTION

VISION

Every day in every way I'm getting better, better and better! I am blessed and highly favored.

GRATITUDE

JOURNAL

On a scale of 1 - 10, How would you rate your effectiveness today? 1 2 3 4 5 6 7 8 9 10

DATE:

Write in complete sentences. i.e "Today I am...", "When I accomplish this..."

WILL

Declaration of intent for the day. What you will do.

OUTCOME

What you will feel when you accomplish this?

OBSTACLES

What could get in the way of you getting these things done?

PLAN & PRAY

What is the plan/how will you make sure it gets done? Then pray on it.

SEE

Imagine your day getting it all done and how it feels (60 seconds)

INTENSION

Who I want to BE today – e.g poised, aware, wise

INVOICE

Do you need to invoice the spirit for anything?

Reading is to the mind what exercise is to the body." - Joseph Addison

DATE:

POWER QUESTION

VISION

Every day in every way I'm getting better, better and better! I am blessed and highly favored.

GRATITUDE

JOURNAL

On a scale of 1 - 10, How would you rate your effectiveness today? 1 2 3 4 5 6 7 8 9 10

DATE:

Write in complete sentences. i.e "Today I am...", "When I accomplish this..."

WILL

Declaration of intent for the day. What you will do.

OUTCOME

What you will feel when you accomplish this?

OBSTACLES

What could get in the way of you getting these things done?

PLAN & PRAY

What is the plan/how will you make sure it gets done? Then pray on it.

SEE

Imagine your day getting it all done and how it feels (60 seconds)

INTENSION

Who I want to BE today – e.g poised, aware, wise

INVOICE

Do you need to invoice the spirit for anything?

"Seeking means: to have a goal; but finding means: to be free, to be receptive, to have no goal."--Herman Hesse

DATE:

POWER QUESTION

VISION

Every day in every way I'm getting better, better and better! I am blessed and highly favored.

GRATITUDE

JOURNAL

On a scale of 1 - 10, How would you rate your effectiveness today? 1 2 3 4 5 6 7 8 9 10

DATE:

Write in complete sentences. i.e "Today I am...", "When I accomplish this..."

WILL

Declaration of intent for the day. What you will do.

OUTCOME

What you will feel when you accomplish this?

OBSTACLES

What could get in the way of you getting these things done?

PLAN & PRAY

What is the plan/how will you make sure it gets done? Then pray on it.

SEE

Imagine your day getting it all done and how it feels (60 seconds)

INTENSION

Who I want to BE today – e.g poised, aware, wise

INVOICE

Do you need to invoice the spirit for anything?

"If you want to test your memory, try to recall what you were worrying about one year ago today." -E.Joseph Coffman

DATE:

POWER QUESTION

VISION

Every day in every way I'm getting better, better and better! I am blessed and highly favored.

GRATITUDE

JOURNAL

On a scale of 1 - 10, How would you rate your effectiveness today? 1 2 3 4 5 6 7 8 9 10

DATE:

Write in complete sentences. i.e "Today I am...", "When I accomplish this..."

WILL

Declaration of intent for the day. What you will do.

OUTCOME

What you will feel when you accomplish this?

OBSTACLES

What could get in the way of you getting these things done?

PLAN & PRAY

What is the plan/how will you make sure it gets done? Then pray on it.

SEE

Imagine your day getting it all done and how it feels (60 seconds)

INTENSION

Who I want to BE today – e.g poised, aware, wise

INVOICE

Do you need to invoice the spirit for anything?

"The key to successful leadership today is influence, not authority." -Kenneth Blanchard

ATE:

POWER QUESTION

VISION

Every day in every way I'm getting better, better and better! I am blessed and highly favored.

GRATITUDE

JOURNAL

On a scale of 1 - 10, How would you rate your effectiveness today? 1 2 3 4 5 6 7 8 9 10

Time for your 30 day check-in P.T.O

DATE:

Big Congrats on making it to 30 days!!!!!!

Revisiting My Why

Use this section to contemplate why you set these goals 30 days ago and how important that still is for you.

Expectations

Review where you expected to be by this point. Are you ahead, on track, behind? Evaluate those results and determine whether ot not you may need to pivot.

DATE:

Effectiveness

Use this section to evaluate you're effectiveness. What is working? What isn't working? How can you do more of what's working and change what is not working?

Next Steps

Write out clearly what your goals are moving forward and where you expect to be in the next 60 day check-in and your 90 day check-in.

DATE:

Write in complete sentences. i.e "Today I am...", "When I accomplish this..."

WILL

Declaration of intent for the day. What you will do.

OUTCOME

What you will feel when you accomplish this?

OBSTACLES

What could get in the way of you getting these things done?

PLAN & PRAY

What is the plan/how will you make sure it gets done? Then pray on it.

SEE

Imagine your day getting it all done and how it feels (60 seconds)

INTENSION

Who I want to BE today – e.g poised, aware, wise

INVOICE

Do you need to invoice the spirit for anything?

"Take care of your body. It's the only place you have to live in." – Jim Rohn

DATE:

POWER QUESTION

VISION

Every day in every way I'm getting better, better and better! I am blessed and highly favored.

GRATITUDE

JOURNAL

On a scale of 1 - 10, How would you rate your effectiveness today? 1 2 3 4 5 6 7 8 9 10

DATE:

Write in complete sentences. i.e "Today I am...", "When I accomplish this..."

WILL

Declaration of intent for the day. What you will do.

OUTCOME

What you will feel when you accomplish this?

OBSTACLES

What could get in the way of you getting these things done?

PLAN & PRAY

What is the plan/how will you make sure it gets done? Then pray on it.

SEE

Imagine your day getting it all done and how it feels (60 seconds)

INTENSION

Who I want to BE today – e.g poised, aware, wise

INVOICE

Do you need to invoice the spirit for anything?

"Exercise should be regarded as a tribute to the heart." - Gene Tunney

DATE:

POWER QUESTION

VISION

Every day in every way I'm getting better, better and better! I am blessed and highly favored.

GRATITUDE

JOURNAL

On a scale of 1 - 10, How would you rate your effectiveness today? 1 2 3 4 5 6 7 8 9 10

DATE:

Write in complete sentences. i.e "Today I am...", "When I accomplish this..."

WILL

Declaration of intent for the day. What you will do.

OUTCOME

What you will feel when you accomplish this?

OBSTACLES

What could get in the way of you getting these things done?

PLAN & PRAY

What is the plan/how will you make sure it gets done? Then pray on it.

SEE

Imagine your day getting it all done and how it feels (60 seconds)

INTENSION

Who I want to BE today – e.g poised, aware, wise

INVOICE

Do you need to invoice the spirit for anything?

"You can't fall if you don't climb. But there's no joy in living your whole life on the ground." - Unknown

DATE:

POWER QUESTION

VISION

Every day in every way I'm getting better, better and better! I am blessed and highly favored.

GRATITUDE

JOURNAL

On a scale of 1 - 10, How would you rate your effectiveness today? 1 2 3 4 5 6 7 8 9 10

DATE:

Write in complete sentences. i.e "Today I am...", "When I accomplish this..."

WILL

Declaration of intent for the day. What you will do.

OUTCOME

What you will feel when you accomplish this?

OBSTACLES

What could get in the way of you getting these things done?

PLAN & PRAY

What is the plan/how will you make sure it gets done? Then pray on it.

SEE

Imagine your day getting it all done and how it feels (60 seconds)

INTENSION

Who I want to BE today – e.g poised, aware, wise

INVOICE

Do you need to invoice the spirit for anything?

"Yes, in all my research, the greatest leaders looked inward and were able to tell a good story with authenticity and passion." - Deepak Chopra

DATE:

POWER QUESTION

VISION

Every day in every way I'm getting better, better and better! I am blessed and highly favored.

GRATITUDE

JOURNAL

On a scale of 1 - 10, How would you rate your effectiveness today? 1 2 3 4 5 6 7 8 9 10

DATE:

Write in complete sentences. i.e "Today I am...", "When I accomplish this..."

WILL

Declaration of intent for the day. What you will do.

OUTCOME

What you will feel when you accomplish this?

OBSTACLES

What could get in the way of you getting these things done?

PLAN & PRAY

What is the plan/how will you make sure it gets done? Then pray on it.

SEE

Imagine your day getting it all done and how it feels (60 seconds)

INTENSION

Who I want to BE today – e.g poised, aware, wise

INVOICE

Do you need to invoice the spirit for anything?

A healthy body is a guest-chamber for the soul; a sick body is a prison." - Francis Bacon

DATE:

POWER QUESTION

VISION

Every day in every way I'm getting better, better and better! I am blessed and highly favored.

GRATITUDE

JOURNAL

On a scale of 1 - 10, How would you rate your effectiveness today? 1 2 3 4 5 6 7 8 9 10

DATE:

Write in complete sentences. i.e "Today I am...", "When I accomplish this..."

WILL

Declaration of intent for the day. What you will do.

OUTCOME

What you will feel when you accomplish this?

OBSTACLES

What could get in the way of you getting these things done?

PLAN & PRAY

What is the plan/how will you make sure it gets done? Then pray on it.

SEE

Imagine your day getting it all done and how it feels (60 seconds)

INTENSION

Who I want to BE today – e.g poised, aware, wise

INVOICE

Do you need to invoice the spirit for anything?

"The strength of the team is each individual member. The strength of each member is the team." --Phil Jackson

DATE:

POWER QUESTION

VISION

Every day in every way I'm getting better, better and better! I am blessed and highly favored.

GRATITUDE

JOURNAL

On a scale of 1 - 10, How would you rate your effectiveness today? 1 2 3 4 5 6 7 8 9 10

DATE:

Write in complete sentences. i.e "Today I am...", "When I accomplish this..."

WILL

Declaration of intent for the day. What you will do.

OUTCOME

What you will feel when you accomplish this?

OBSTACLES

What could get in the way of you getting these things done?

PLAN & PRAY

What is the plan/how will you make sure it gets done? Then pray on it.

SEE

Imagine your day getting it all done and how it feels (60 seconds)

INTENSION

Who I want to BE today – e.g poised, aware, wise

INVOICE

Do you need to invoice the spirit for anything?

"When I meet successful people I ask 100 questions as to what they attribute their success to. It is usually the same: persistence, hard work and hiring good people." -Kiana Tom

DATE:

POWER QUESTION

VISION

Every day in every way I'm getting better, better and better! I am blessed and highly favored.

GRATITUDE

JOURNAL

On a scale of 1 - 10, How would you rate your effectiveness today? 1 2 3 4 5 6 7 8 9 10

DATE:

Write in complete sentences. i.e "Today I am...", "When I accomplish this..."

WILL

Declaration of intent for the day. What you will do.

OUTCOME

What you will feel when you accomplish this?

OBSTACLES

What could get in the way of you getting these things done?

PLAN & PRAY

What is the plan/how will you make sure it gets done? Then pray on it.

SEE

Imagine your day getting it all done and how it feels (60 seconds)

INTENSION

Who I want to BE today – e.g poised, aware, wise

INVOICE

Do you need to invoice the spirit for anything?

"A happy family is but an earlier heaven." -George Bernard Shaw

DATE:

POWER QUESTION

VISION

Every day in every way I'm getting better, better and better! I am blessed and highly favored.

GRATITUDE

JOURNAL

On a scale of 1 - 10, How would you rate your effectiveness today? 1 2 3 4 5 6 7 8 9 10

DATE:

Write in complete sentences. i.e "Today I am...", "When I accomplish this..."

WILL

Declaration of intent for the day. What you will do.

OUTCOME

What you will feel when you accomplish this?

OBSTACLES

What could get in the way of you getting these things done?

PLAN & PRAY

What is the plan/how will you make sure it gets done? Then pray on it.

SEE

Imagine your day getting it all done and how it feels (60 seconds)

INTENSION

Who I want to BE today – e.g poised, aware, wise

INVOICE

Do you need to invoice the spirit for anything?

"The things you do for yourself are gone when you are gone, but the things you do for others remain as your legacy." -Kalu Ndukwe Kalu

DATE:

POWER QUESTION

VISION

Every day in every way I'm getting better, better and better! I am blessed and highly favored.

GRATITUDE

JOURNAL

On a scale of 1 - 10, How would you rate your effectiveness today? 1 2 3 4 5 6 7 8 9 10

DATE:

Write in complete sentences. i.e "Today I am...", "When I accomplish this..."

WILL

Declaration of intent for the day. What you will do.

OUTCOME

What you will feel when you accomplish this?

OBSTACLES

What could get in the way of you getting these things done?

PLAN & PRAY

What is the plan/how will you make sure it gets done? Then pray on it.

SEE

Imagine your day getting it all done and how it feels (60 seconds)

INTENSION

Who I want to BE today – e.g poised, aware, wise

INVOICE

Do you need to invoice the spirit for anything?

We are what we repeatedly do. Excellence, then, is not an act, but a habit." – Will Durant

DATE:

POWER QUESTION

VISION

Every day in every way I'm getting better, better and better! I am blessed and highly favored.

GRATITUDE

JOURNAL

On a scale of 1 - 10, How would you rate your effectiveness today? 1 2 3 4 5 6 7 8 9 10

DATE:

Write in complete sentences. i.e "Today I am...", "When I accomplish this..."

WILL

Declaration of intent for the day. What you will do.

OUTCOME

What you will feel when you accomplish this?

OBSTACLES

What could get in the way of you getting these things done?

PLAN & PRAY

What is the plan/how will you make sure it gets done? Then pray on it.

SEE

Imagine your day getting it all done and how it feels (60 seconds)

INTENSION

Who I want to BE today – e.g poised, aware, wise

INVOICE

Do you need to invoice the spirit for anything?

"Learn to adjust yourself to the conditions you have to endure, but make a point of trying to alter or correct conditions so that they are most favorable to you." - William Frederick Book

DATE:

POWER QUESTION

VISION

Every day in every way I'm getting better, better and better! I am blessed and highly favored.

GRATITUDE

JOURNAL

On a scale of 1 - 10, How would you rate your effectiveness today? 1 2 3 4 5 6 7 8 9 10

DATE:

Write in complete sentences. i.e "Today I am...", "When I accomplish this..."

WILL

Declaration of intent for the day. What you will do.

OUTCOME

What you will feel when you accomplish this?

OBSTACLES

What could get in the way of you getting these things done?

PLAN & PRAY

What is the plan/how will you make sure it gets done? Then pray on it.

SEE

Imagine your day getting it all done and how it feels (60 seconds)

INTENSION

Who I want to BE today – e.g poised, aware, wise

INVOICE

Do you need to invoice the spirit for anything?

"A sad soul can be just as lethal as a germ." - John Steinbeck

DATE:

POWER QUESTION

VISION

Every day in every way I'm getting better, better and better! I am blessed and highly favored.

GRATITUDE

JOURNAL

On a scale of 1 - 10, How would you rate your effectiveness today? 1 2 3 4 5 6 7 8 9 10

DATE:

Write in complete sentences. i.e "Today I am...", "When I accomplish this..."

WILL

Declaration of intent for the day. What you will do.

OUTCOME

What you will feel when you accomplish this?

OBSTACLES

What could get in the way of you getting these things done?

PLAN & PRAY

What is the plan/how will you make sure it gets done? Then pray on it.

SEE

Imagine your day getting it all done and how it feels (60 seconds)

INTENSION

Who I want to BE today – e.g poised, aware, wise

INVOICE

Do you need to invoice the spirit for anything?

"Simplicity is not the goal. It is the by-product of a good idea and modest expectations." - Paul Rand

DATE:

POWER QUESTION

VISION

Every day in every way I'm getting better, better and better! I am blessed and highly favored.

GRATITUDE

JOURNAL

On a scale of 1 - 10, How would you rate your effectiveness today? 1 2 3 4 5 6 7 8 9 10

DATE:

Write in complete sentences. i.e "Today I am...", "When I accomplish this..."

WILL

Declaration of intent for the day. What you will do.

OUTCOME

What you will feel when you accomplish this?

OBSTACLES

What could get in the way of you getting these things done?

PLAN & PRAY

What is the plan/how will you make sure it gets done? Then pray on it.

SEE

Imagine your day getting it all done and how it feels (60 seconds)

INTENSION

Who I want to BE today – e.g poised, aware, wise

INVOICE

Do you need to invoice the spirit for anything?

"Management is nothing more than motivating other people." -Lee Iacocca

DATE:

POWER QUESTION

VISION

Every day in every way I'm getting better, better and better! I am blessed and highly favored.

GRATITUDE

JOURNAL

On a scale of 1 - 10, How would you rate your effectiveness today? 1 2 3 4 5 6 7 8 9 10

DATE:

Write in complete sentences. i.e "Today I am...", "When I accomplish this..."

WILL

Declaration of intent for the day. What you will do.

OUTCOME

What you will feel when you accomplish this?

OBSTACLES

What could get in the way of you getting these things done?

PLAN & PRAY

What is the plan/how will you make sure it gets done? Then pray on it.

SEE

Imagine your day getting it all done and how it feels (60 seconds)

INTENSION

Who I want to BE today – e.g poised, aware, wise

INVOICE

Do you need to invoice the spirit for anything?

"The slogans "hang on" and "press on" have solved and will continue to solve the problems of humanity." -Ogwo David Emenike

ATE:

POWER QUESTION

VISION

Every day in every way I'm getting better, better and better! I am blessed and highly favored.

GRATITUDE

JOURNAL

On a scale of 1 - 10, How would you rate your effectiveness today? 1 2 3 4 5 6 7 8 9 10

DATE:

Write in complete sentences. i.e "Today I am...", "When I accomplish this..."

WILL

Declaration of intent for the day. What you will do.

OUTCOME

What you will feel when you accomplish this?

OBSTACLES

What could get in the way of you getting these things done?

PLAN & PRAY

What is the plan/how will you make sure it gets done? Then pray on it.

SEE

Imagine your day getting it all done and how it feels (60 seconds)

INTENSION

Who I want to BE today – e.g poised, aware, wise

INVOICE

Do you need to invoice the spirit for anything?

"I know for sure that what we dwell on is who we become." -Oprah Winfrey

DATE:

POWER QUESTION

VISION

Every day in every way I'm getting better, better and better! I am blessed and highly favored.

GRATITUDE

JOURNAL

On a scale of 1 - 10, How would you rate your effectiveness today? 1 2 3 4 5 6 7 8 9 10

DATE:

Write in complete sentences. i.e "Today I am...", "When I accomplish this..."

WILL

Declaration of intent for the day. What you will do.

OUTCOME

What you will feel when you accomplish this?

OBSTACLES

What could get in the way of you getting these things done?

PLAN & PRAY

What is the plan/how will you make sure it gets done? Then pray on it.

SEE

Imagine your day getting it all done and how it feels (60 seconds)

INTENSION

Who I want to BE today – e.g poised, aware, wise

INVOICE

Do you need to invoice the spirit for anything?

"All fixed set patterns are incapable of adaptability or pliability. The truth is outside of all fixed patterns." ~ Bruce Lee

DATE:

POWER QUESTION

VISION

Every day in every way I'm getting better, better and better! I am blessed and highly favored.

GRATITUDE

JOURNAL

On a scale of 1 - 10, How would you rate your effectiveness today? 1 2 3 4 5 6 7 8 9 10

DATE:

Write in complete sentences. i.e "Today I am...", "When I accomplish this..."

WILL

Declaration of intent for the day. What you will do.

OUTCOME

What you will feel when you accomplish this?

OBSTACLES

What could get in the way of you getting these things done?

PLAN & PRAY

What is the plan/how will you make sure it gets done? Then pray on it.

SEE

Imagine your day getting it all done and how it feels (60 seconds)

INTENSION

Who I want to BE today – e.g poised, aware, wise

INVOICE

Do you need to invoice the spirit for anything?

"What you do speaks so loudly that I cannot hear what you say." -Ralph Waldo Emerson

POWER QUESTION

VISION

Every day in every way I'm getting better, better and better! I am blessed and highly favored.

GRATITUDE

JOURNAL

On a scale of 1 - 10, How would you rate your effectiveness today? 1 2 3 4 5 6 7 8 9 10

DATE:

Write in complete sentences. i.e "Today I am...", "When I accomplish this..."

WILL

Declaration of intent for the day. What you will do.

OUTCOME

What you will feel when you accomplish this?

OBSTACLES

What could get in the way of you getting these things done?

PLAN & PRAY

What is the plan/how will you make sure it gets done? Then pray on it.

SEE

Imagine your day getting it all done and how it feels (60 seconds)

INTENSION

Who I want to BE today – e.g poised, aware, wise

INVOICE

Do you need to invoice the spirit for anything?

"We are only as strong as we are united, as weak as we are divided." -J.K. Rowling

DATE:

POWER QUESTION

VISION

Every day in every way I'm getting better, better and better! I am blessed and highly favored.

GRATITUDE

JOURNAL

On a scale of 1 - 10, How would you rate your effectiveness today? 1 2 3 4 5 6 7 8 9 10

DATE:

Write in complete sentences. i.e "Today I am...", "When I accomplish this..."

WILL

Declaration of intent for the day. What you will do.

OUTCOME

What you will feel when you accomplish this?

OBSTACLES

What could get in the way of you getting these things done?

PLAN & PRAY

What is the plan/how will you make sure it gets done? Then pray on it.

SEE

Imagine your day getting it all done and how it feels (60 seconds)

INTENSION

Who I want to BE today – e.g poised, aware, wise

INVOICE

Do you need to invoice the spirit for anything?

"You cannot truly listen to anyone and do anything else at the same time." -M. Scott Peck

DATE:

POWER QUESTION

VISION

Every day in every way I'm getting better, better and better! I am blessed and highly favored.

GRATITUDE

JOURNAL

On a scale of 1 - 10, How would you rate your effectiveness today? 1 2 3 4 5 6 7 8 9 10

DATE:

Write in complete sentences. i.e "Today I am...", "When I accomplish this..."

WILL

Declaration of intent for the day. What you will do.

OUTCOME

What you will feel when you accomplish this?

OBSTACLES

What could get in the way of you getting these things done?

PLAN & PRAY

What is the plan/how will you make sure it gets done? Then pray on it.

SEE

Imagine your day getting it all done and how it feels (60 seconds)

INTENSION

Who I want to BE today – e.g poised, aware, wise

INVOICE

Do you need to invoice the spirit for anything?

"It is obvious that we can no more explain a passion to a person who has never experienced it than we can explain light to the blind."--T. S. Eliot

DATE:

POWER QUESTION

VISION

Every day in every way I'm getting better, better and better! I am blessed and highly favored.

GRATITUDE

JOURNAL

On a scale of 1 - 10, How would you rate your effectiveness today? 1 2 3 4 5 6 7 8 9 10

DATE:

Write in complete sentences. i.e "Today I am...", "When I accomplish this..."

WILL

Declaration of intent for the day. What you will do.

OUTCOME

What you will feel when you accomplish this?

OBSTACLES

What could get in the way of you getting these things done?

PLAN & PRAY

What is the plan/how will you make sure it gets done? Then pray on it.

SEE

Imagine your day getting it all done and how it feels (60 seconds)

INTENSION

Who I want to BE today – e.g poised, aware, wise

INVOICE

Do you need to invoice the spirit for anything?

"Do you want to know who you are? Don't ask. Act! Action will delineate and define you." Thomas Jefferson

ATE:

POWER QUESTION

VISION

Every day in every way I'm getting better, better and better! I am blessed and highly favored.

GRATITUDE

JOURNAL

On a scale of 1 - 10, How would you rate your effectiveness today? 1 2 3 4 5 6 7 8 9 10

DATE:

Write in complete sentences. i.e "Today I am...", "When I accomplish this..."

WILL

Declaration of intent for the day. What you will do.

OUTCOME

What you will feel when you accomplish this?

OBSTACLES

What could get in the way of you getting these things done?

PLAN & PRAY

What is the plan/how will you make sure it gets done? Then pray on it.

SEE

Imagine your day getting it all done and how it feels (60 seconds)

INTENSION

Who I want to BE today – e.g poised, aware, wise

INVOICE

Do you need to invoice the spirit for anything?

"Nourishing yourself in a way that helps you blossom in the direction you want to go is attainable and you are worth the effort." - Deborah Day

ATE:

POWER QUESTION

VISION

Every day in every way I'm getting better, better and better! I am blessed and highly favored.

GRATITUDE

JOURNAL

On a scale of 1 - 10, How would you rate your effectiveness today? 1 2 3 4 5 6 7 8 9 10

DATE:

Write in complete sentences. i.e "Today I am...", "When I accomplish this..."

WILL

Declaration of intent for the day. What you will do.

OUTCOME

What you will feel when you accomplish this?

OBSTACLES

What could get in the way of you getting these things done?

PLAN & PRAY

What is the plan/how will you make sure it gets done? Then pray on it.

SEE

Imagine your day getting it all done and how it feels (60 seconds)

INTENSION

Who I want to BE today – e.g poised, aware, wise

INVOICE

Do you need to invoice the spirit for anything?

It is the soul's duty to be loyal to its own desires. It must abandon itself to its master passion. -Rebecca West

ATE:

POWER QUESTION

VISION

Every day in every way I'm getting better, better and better! I am blessed and highly favored.

GRATITUDE

JOURNAL

On a scale of 1 - 10, How would you rate your effectiveness today? 1 2 3 4 5 6 7 8 9 10

DATE:

Write in complete sentences. i.e "Today I am...", "When I accomplish this..."

WILL

Declaration of intent for the day. What you will do.

OUTCOME

What you will feel when you accomplish this?

OBSTACLES

What could get in the way of you getting these things done?

PLAN & PRAY

What is the plan/how will you make sure it gets done? Then pray on it.

SEE

Imagine your day getting it all done and how it feels (60 seconds)

INTENSION

Who I want to BE today – e.g poised, aware, wise

INVOICE

Do you need to invoice the spirit for anything?

"To ensure good health: eat lightly, breathe deeply, live moderately, cultivate cheerfulness, and maintain an interest in life." - William Londen

ATE:

POWER QUESTION

VISION

Every day in every way I'm getting better, better and better! I am blessed and highly favored.

GRATITUDE

JOURNAL

On a scale of 1 - 10, How would you rate your effectiveness today? 1 2 3 4 5 6 7 8 9 10

DATE:

Write in complete sentences. i.e "Today I am...", "When I accomplish this..."

WILL

Declaration of intent for the day. What you will do.

OUTCOME

What you will feel when you accomplish this?

OBSTACLES

What could get in the way of you getting these things done?

PLAN & PRAY

What is the plan/how will you make sure it gets done? Then pray on it.

SEE

Imagine your day getting it all done and how it feels (60 seconds)

INTENSION

Who I want to BE today – e.g poised, aware, wise

INVOICE

Do you need to invoice the spirit for anything?

"Reflect upon your present blessings--of which every man has many--not on your past misfortunes, of which all men have some." -Charles Dickens,

ATE:

POWER QUESTION

VISION

Every day in every way I'm getting better, better and better! I am blessed and highly favored.

GRATITUDE

JOURNAL

On a scale of 1 - 10, How would you rate your effectiveness today? 1 2 3 4 5 6 7 8 9 10

DATE:

Write in complete sentences. i.e "Today I am...", "When I accomplish this..."

WILL

Declaration of intent for the day. What you will do.

OUTCOME

What you will feel when you accomplish this?

OBSTACLES

What could get in the way of you getting these things done?

PLAN & PRAY

What is the plan/how will you make sure it gets done? Then pray on it.

SEE

Imagine your day getting it all done and how it feels (60 seconds)

INTENSION

Who I want to BE today – e.g poised, aware, wise

INVOICE

Do you need to invoice the spirit for anything?

"Humility is throwing oneself away in complete concentration on something or someone else." Madeleine L'Engle

ATE:

POWER QUESTION

VISION

Every day in every way I'm getting better, better and better! I am blessed and highly favored.

GRATITUDE

JOURNAL

On a scale of 1 - 10, How would you rate your effectiveness today? 1 2 3 4 5 6 7 8 9 10

DATE:

Write in complete sentences. i.e "Today I am...", "When I accomplish this..."

WILL

Declaration of intent for the day. What you will do.

OUTCOME

What you will feel when you accomplish this?

OBSTACLES

What could get in the way of you getting these things done?

PLAN & PRAY

What is the plan/how will you make sure it gets done? Then pray on it.

SEE

Imagine your day getting it all done and how it feels (60 seconds)

INTENSION

Who I want to BE today – e.g poised, aware, wise

INVOICE

Do you need to invoice the spirit for anything?

Make eating fruits and vegetables a priority. This is so simple and beneficial, yet most people don't do it." - Nia Shanks

ATE:

POWER QUESTION

VISION

Every day in every way I'm getting better, better and better! I am blessed and highly favored.

GRATITUDE

JOURNAL

On a scale of 1 - 10, How would you rate your effectiveness today? 1 2 3 4 5 6 7 8 9 10

DATE:

Write in complete sentences. i.e "Today I am...", "When I accomplish this..."

WILL

Declaration of intent for the day. What you will do.

OUTCOME

What you will feel when you accomplish this?

OBSTACLES

What could get in the way of you getting these things done?

PLAN & PRAY

What is the plan/how will you make sure it gets done? Then pray on it.

SEE

Imagine your day getting it all done and how it feels (60 seconds)

INTENSION

Who I want to BE today – e.g poised, aware, wise

INVOICE

Do you need to invoice the spirit for anything?

"Fall seven times and stand up eight." -Japanese Proverb

ATE:

POWER QUESTION

VISION

Every day in every way I'm getting better, better and better! I am blessed and highly favored.

GRATITUDE

JOURNAL

On a scale of 1 - 10, How would you rate your effectiveness today? 1 2 3 4 5 6 7 8 9 10

DATE:

Write in complete sentences. i.e "Today I am...", "When I accomplish this..."

WILL

Declaration of intent for the day. What you will do.

OUTCOME

What you will feel when you accomplish this?

OBSTACLES

What could get in the way of you getting these things done?

PLAN & PRAY

What is the plan/how will you make sure it gets done? Then pray on it.

SEE

Imagine your day getting it all done and how it feels (60 seconds)

INTENSION

Who I want to BE today – e.g poised, aware, wise

INVOICE

Do you need to invoice the spirit for anything?

"Thank you' is the best prayer that anyone could say. I say that one a lot. Thank you expresses extreme gratitude, humility, understanding." -Alice Walker

ATE:

POWER QUESTION

VISION

Every day in every way I'm getting better, better and better! I am blessed and highly favored.

GRATITUDE

JOURNAL

On a scale of 1 - 10, How would you rate your effectiveness today? 1 2 3 4 5 6 7 8 9 10

Time for your 60 day check-in P.T.O

DATE:

Big Congrats on making it to 60 days!!!!!!

Revisiting My Why

Use this section to contemplate why you set these goals 30 days ago and how important that still is for you.

Expectations

Review where you expected to be by this point. Are you ahead, on track, behind? Evaluate those results and determine whether ot not you may need to pivot.

ATE:

Effectiveness

Jse this section to evaluate you're effectiveness. What is working? What isn't working? Iow can you do more of what's working and change what is not working?

Next Steps

Vrite out clearly what your goals are moving forward and where you expect to be in the next 90 day check-in.

DATE:

Write in complete sentences. i.e "Today I am...", "When I accomplish this..."

WILL

Declaration of intent for the day. What you will do.

OUTCOME

What you will feel when you accomplish this?

OBSTACLES

What could get in the way of you getting these things done?

PLAN & PRAY

What is the plan/how will you make sure it gets done? Then pray on it.

SEE

Imagine your day getting it all done and how it feels (60 seconds)

INTENSION

Who I want to BE today – e.g poised, aware, wise

INVOICE

Do you need to invoice the spirit for anything?

"Yes, in all my research, the greatest leaders looked inward and were able to tell a good story with authenticity and passion." --Deepak Chopra

ATE:

POWER QUESTION

VISION

Every day in every way I'm getting better, better and better! I am blessed and highly favored.

GRATITUDE

JOURNAL

On a scale of 1 - 10, How would you rate your effectiveness today? 1 2 3 4 5 6 7 8 9 10

DATE:

Write in complete sentences. i.e "Today I am...", "When I accomplish this..."

WILL

Declaration of intent for the day. What you will do.

OUTCOME

What you will feel when you accomplish this?

OBSTACLES

What could get in the way of you getting these things done?

PLAN & PRAY

What is the plan/how will you make sure it gets done? Then pray on it.

SEE

Imagine your day getting it all done and how it feels (60 seconds)

INTENSION

Who I want to BE today – e.g poised, aware, wise

INVOICE

Do you need to invoice the spirit for anything?

"Authentic brands don't emerge from marketing cubicles or advertising agencies. They emanate from everything the company does..." --Howard Schultz

ATE:

POWER QUESTION

VISION

Every day in every way I'm getting better, better and better! I am blessed and highly favored.

GRATITUDE

JOURNAL

On a scale of 1 - 10, How would you rate your effectiveness today? 1 2 3 4 5 6 7 8 9 10

DATE:

Write in complete sentences. i.e "Today I am...", "When I accomplish this..."

WILL

Declaration of intent for the day. What you will do.

OUTCOME

What you will feel when you accomplish this?

OBSTACLES

What could get in the way of you getting these things done?

PLAN & PRAY

What is the plan/how will you make sure it gets done? Then pray on it.

SEE

Imagine your day getting it all done and how it feels (60 seconds)

INTENSION

Who I want to BE today – e.g poised, aware, wise

INVOICE

Do you need to invoice the spirit for anything?

"Even the smallest act of caring for another person is like a drop of water -it will make ripples throughout the entire pond..." -Jessy and Bryan Matteo

ATE:

POWER QUESTION

VISION

Every day in every way I'm getting better, better and better! I am blessed and highly favored.

GRATITUDE

JOURNAL

On a scale of 1 - 10, How would you rate your effectiveness today? 1 2 3 4 5 6 7 8 9 10

DATE:

Write in complete sentences. i.e "Today I am...", "When I accomplish this..."

WILL

Declaration of intent for the day. What you will do.

OUTCOME

What you will feel when you accomplish this?

OBSTACLES

What could get in the way of you getting these things done?

PLAN & PRAY

What is the plan/how will you make sure it gets done? Then pray on it.

SEE

Imagine your day getting it all done and how it feels (60 seconds)

INTENSION

Who I want to BE today – e.g poised, aware, wise

INVOICE

Do you need to invoice the spirit for anything?

"Wellness is a connection of paths: knowledge and action." - Joshua Holtz

ATE:

POWER QUESTION

VISION

Every day in every way I'm getting better, better and better! I am blessed and highly favored.

GRATITUDE

JOURNAL

On a scale of 1 - 10, How would you rate your effectiveness today? 1 2 3 4 5 6 7 8 9 10

DATE:

Write in complete sentences. i.e "Today I am...", "When I accomplish this..."

WILL

Declaration of intent for the day. What you will do.

OUTCOME

What you will feel when you accomplish this?

OBSTACLES

What could get in the way of you getting these things done?

PLAN & PRAY

What is the plan/how will you make sure it gets done? Then pray on it.

SEE

Imagine your day getting it all done and how it feels (60 seconds)

INTENSION

Who I want to BE today – e.g poised, aware, wise

INVOICE

Do you need to invoice the spirit for anything?

"Health is a state of complete mental, social and physical well-being, not merely the absence of disease or infirmity." - World Health Organization, 1948

ATE:

POWER QUESTION

VISION

Every day in every way I'm getting better, better and better! I am blessed and highly favored.

GRATITUDE

JOURNAL

On a scale of 1 - 10, How would you rate your effectiveness today? 1 2 3 4 5 6 7 8 9 10

DATE:

Write in complete sentences. i.e "Today I am...", "When I accomplish this..."

WILL

Declaration of intent for the day. What you will do.

OUTCOME

What you will feel when you accomplish this?

OBSTACLES

What could get in the way of you getting these things done?

PLAN & PRAY

What is the plan/how will you make sure it gets done? Then pray on it.

SEE

Imagine your day getting it all done and how it feels (60 seconds)

INTENSION

Who I want to BE today – e.g poised, aware, wise

INVOICE

Do you need to invoice the spirit for anything?

"Let gratitude be the pillow upon which you kneel to say your nightly prayer. And let faith be the bridge you build to overcome evil and welcome good."
Maya Angelou, Celebrations: Rituals of Peace and Prayer

ATE:

POWER QUESTION

VISION

Every day in every way I'm getting better, better and better! I am blessed and highly favored.

GRATITUDE

JOURNAL

On a scale of 1 - 10, How would you rate your effectiveness today? 1 2 3 4 5 6 7 8 9 10

DATE:

Write in complete sentences. i.e "Today I am...", "When I accomplish this..."

WILL

Declaration of intent for the day. What you will do.

OUTCOME

What you will feel when you accomplish this?

OBSTACLES

What could get in the way of you getting these things done?

PLAN & PRAY

What is the plan/how will you make sure it gets done? Then pray on it.

SEE

Imagine your day getting it all done and how it feels (60 seconds)

INTENSION

Who I want to BE today – e.g poised, aware, wise

INVOICE

Do you need to invoice the spirit for anything?

"To improve is to change; to be perfect is to change often." - Winston Churchill

ATE:

POWER QUESTION

VISION

Every day in every way I'm getting better, better and better! I am blessed and highly favored.

GRATITUDE

JOURNAL

On a scale of 1 - 10, How would you rate your effectiveness today? 1 2 3 4 5 6 7 8 9 10

DATE:

Write in complete sentences. i.e "Today I am...", "When I accomplish this..."

WILL

Declaration of intent for the day. What you will do.

OUTCOME

What you will feel when you accomplish this?

OBSTACLES

What could get in the way of you getting these things done?

PLAN & PRAY

What is the plan/how will you make sure it gets done? Then pray on it.

SEE

Imagine your day getting it all done and how it feels (60 seconds)

INTENSION

Who I want to BE today – e.g poised, aware, wise

INVOICE

Do you need to invoice the spirit for anything?

"It is health that is the real wealth, and not pieces of gold and silver." -Mahatma Gandhi

ATE:

POWER QUESTION

VISION

Every day in every way I'm getting better, better and better! I am blessed and highly favored.

GRATITUDE

JOURNAL

On a scale of 1 - 10, How would you rate your effectiveness today? 1 2 3 4 5 6 7 8 9 10

DATE:

Write in complete sentences. i.e "Today I am...", "When I accomplish this..."

WILL

Declaration of intent for the day. What you will do.

OUTCOME

What you will feel when you accomplish this?

OBSTACLES

What could get in the way of you getting these things done?

PLAN & PRAY

What is the plan/how will you make sure it gets done? Then pray on it.

SEE

Imagine your day getting it all done and how it feels (60 seconds)

INTENSION

Who I want to BE today – e.g poised, aware, wise

INVOICE

Do you need to invoice the spirit for anything?

"Real genius is nothing else but the supernatural virtue of humility in the domain of thought." -Simone Weil

ATE:

POWER QUESTION

VISION

Every day in every way I'm getting better, better and better! I am blessed and highly favored.

GRATITUDE

JOURNAL

On a scale of 1 - 10, How would you rate your effectiveness today? 1 2 3 4 5 6 7 8 9 10

DATE:

Write in complete sentences. i.e "Today I am...", "When I accomplish this..."

WILL

Declaration of intent for the day. What you will do.

OUTCOME

What you will feel when you accomplish this?

OBSTACLES

What could get in the way of you getting these things done?

PLAN & PRAY

What is the plan/how will you make sure it gets done? Then pray on it.

SEE

Imagine your day getting it all done and how it feels (60 seconds)

INTENSION

Who I want to BE today – e.g poised, aware, wise

INVOICE

Do you need to invoice the spirit for anything?

"You are born into your family and your family is born into you. No returns. No exchanges." -Elizabeth Berg

ATE:

POWER QUESTION

VISION

Every day in every way I'm getting better, better and better! I am blessed and highly favored.

GRATITUDE

JOURNAL

On a scale of 1 - 10, How would you rate your effectiveness today? 1 2 3 4 5 6 7 8 9 10

DATE:

Write in complete sentences. i.e "Today I am...", "When I accomplish this..."

WILL

Declaration of intent for the day. What you will do.

OUTCOME

What you will feel when you accomplish this?

OBSTACLES

What could get in the way of you getting these things done?

PLAN & PRAY

What is the plan/how will you make sure it gets done? Then pray on it.

SEE

Imagine your day getting it all done and how it feels (60 seconds)

INTENSION

Who I want to BE today – e.g poised, aware, wise

INVOICE

Do you need to invoice the spirit for anything?

We do not stop exercising because we grow old-we grow old because we stop exercising."
- Dr. Kenneth Cooper

ATE:

POWER QUESTION

VISION

Every day in every way I'm getting better, better and better! I am blessed and highly favored.

GRATITUDE

JOURNAL

On a scale of 1 - 10, How would you rate your effectiveness today? 1 2 3 4 5 6 7 8 9 10

DATE:

Write in complete sentences. i.e "Today I am...", "When I accomplish this..."

WILL

Declaration of intent for the day. What you will do.

OUTCOME

What you will feel when you accomplish this?

OBSTACLES

What could get in the way of you getting these things done?

PLAN & PRAY

What is the plan/how will you make sure it gets done? Then pray on it.

SEE

Imagine your day getting it all done and how it feels (60 seconds)

INTENSION

Who I want to BE today – e.g poised, aware, wise

INVOICE

Do you need to invoice the spirit for anything?

"When I let go of what I am, I become what I might be." -Lao Tzu

ATE:

POWER QUESTION

VISION

Every day in every way I'm getting better, better and better! I am blessed and highly favored.

GRATITUDE

JOURNAL

On a scale of 1 - 10, How would you rate your effectiveness today? 1 2 3 4 5 6 7 8 9 10

DATE:

Write in complete sentences. i.e "Today I am...", "When I accomplish this..."

WILL

Declaration of intent for the day. What you will do.

OUTCOME

What you will feel when you accomplish this?

OBSTACLES

What could get in the way of you getting these things done?

PLAN & PRAY

What is the plan/how will you make sure it gets done? Then pray on it.

SEE

Imagine your day getting it all done and how it feels (60 seconds)

INTENSION

Who I want to BE today – e.g poised, aware, wise

INVOICE

Do you need to invoice the spirit for anything?

Only the disciplined are truly free. The undisciplined are slaves to moods, appetites and passions." - Stephen Covey

ATE:

POWER QUESTION

VISION

Every day in every way I'm getting better, better and better! I am blessed and highly favored.

GRATITUDE

JOURNAL

On a scale of 1 - 10, How would you rate your effectiveness today? 1 2 3 4 5 6 7 8 9 10

DATE:

Write in complete sentences. i.e "Today I am...", "When I accomplish this..."

WILL

Declaration of intent for the day. What you will do.

OUTCOME

What you will feel when you accomplish this?

OBSTACLES

What could get in the way of you getting these things done?

PLAN & PRAY

What is the plan/how will you make sure it gets done? Then pray on it.

SEE

Imagine your day getting it all done and how it feels (60 seconds)

INTENSION

Who I want to BE today – e.g poised, aware, wise

INVOICE

Do you need to invoice the spirit for anything?

"It is impossible to withhold education from the receptive mind, as it is impossible to force it upon the unreasoning." -Agnes Repplier

ATE:

POWER QUESTION

VISION

Every day in every way I'm getting better, better and better! I am blessed and highly favored.

GRATITUDE

JOURNAL

On a scale of 1 - 10, How would you rate your effectiveness today? 1 2 3 4 5 6 7 8 9 10

DATE:

Write in complete sentences. i.e "Today I am...", "When I accomplish this..."

WILL

Declaration of intent for the day. What you will do.

OUTCOME

What you will feel when you accomplish this?

OBSTACLES

What could get in the way of you getting these things done?

PLAN & PRAY

What is the plan/how will you make sure it gets done? Then pray on it.

SEE

Imagine your day getting it all done and how it feels (60 seconds)

INTENSION

Who I want to BE today – e.g poised, aware, wise

INVOICE

Do you need to invoice the spirit for anything?

"Keeping your body healthy is an expression of gratitude to the whole cosmos- the trees, the clouds, everything." - Thích Nhat Hanh

ATE:

POWER QUESTION

VISION

Every day in every way I'm getting better, better and better! I am blessed and highly favored.

GRATITUDE

JOURNAL

On a scale of 1 - 10, How would you rate your effectiveness today? 1 2 3 4 5 6 7 8 9 10

may want to pre-order you new journal now so it arrives in time for your next 90-days

DATE:

Write in complete sentences. i.e "Today I am...", "When I accomplish this..."

WILL

Declaration of intent for the day. What you will do.

OUTCOME

What you will feel when you accomplish this?

OBSTACLES

What could get in the way of you getting these things done?

PLAN & PRAY

What is the plan/how will you make sure it gets done? Then pray on it.

SEE

Imagine your day getting it all done and how it feels (60 seconds)

INTENSION

Who I want to BE today – e.g poised, aware, wise

INVOICE

Do you need to invoice the spirit for anything?

"If you feel like there's something out there that you're supposed to be doing, if you have a passion for it, then stop WILLing and just do it." - Wanda Skyes

ATE:

POWER QUESTION

VISION

Every day in every way I'm getting better, better and better! I am blessed and highly favored.

GRATITUDE

JOURNAL

On a scale of 1 - 10, How would you rate your effectiveness today? 1 2 3 4 5 6 7 8 9 10

DATE:

Write in complete sentences. i.e "Today I am...", "When I accomplish this..."

WILL

Declaration of intent for the day. What you will do.

OUTCOME

What you will feel when you accomplish this?

OBSTACLES

What could get in the way of you getting these things done?

PLAN & PRAY

What is the plan/how will you make sure it gets done? Then pray on it.

SEE

Imagine your day getting it all done and how it feels (60 seconds)

INTENSION

Who I want to BE today – e.g poised, aware, wise

INVOICE

Do you need to invoice the spirit for anything?

"As long as we are persistence in our pursuit of our deepest destiny, we will continue to grow. We cannot choose the day or time when we will fully bloom. It happens in its own time." - Denis Waitley

ATE:

POWER QUESTION

VISION

Every day in every way I'm getting better, better and better! I am blessed and highly favored.

GRATITUDE

JOURNAL

On a scale of 1 - 10, How would you rate your effectiveness today? 1 2 3 4 5 6 7 8 9 10

DATE:

Write in complete sentences. i.e "Today I am...", "When I accomplish this..."

WILL

Declaration of intent for the day. What you will do.

OUTCOME

What you will feel when you accomplish this?

OBSTACLES

What could get in the way of you getting these things done?

PLAN & PRAY

What is the plan/how will you make sure it gets done? Then pray on it.

SEE

Imagine your day getting it all done and how it feels (60 seconds)

INTENSION

Who I want to BE today – e.g poised, aware, wise

INVOICE

Do you need to invoice the spirit for anything?

"The world breaks every one and afterward many are strong at the broken places." - Ernest Hemingway

ATE:

POWER QUESTION

VISION

Every day in every way I'm getting better, better and better! I am blessed and highly favored.

GRATITUDE

JOURNAL

On a scale of 1 - 10, How would you rate your effectiveness today? 1 2 3 4 5 6 7 8 9 10

DATE:

Write in complete sentences. i.e "Today I am...", "When I accomplish this..."

WILL

Declaration of intent for the day. What you will do.

OUTCOME

What you will feel when you accomplish this?

OBSTACLES

What could get in the way of you getting these things done?

PLAN & PRAY

What is the plan/how will you make sure it gets done? Then pray on it.

SEE

Imagine your day getting it all done and how it feels (60 seconds)

INTENSION

Who I want to BE today – e.g poised, aware, wise

INVOICE

Do you need to invoice the spirit for anything?

"Management is efficiency in climbing the ladder of success; leadership determines whether the ladder is leaning against the right wall." -Stephen Covey

ATE:

POWER QUESTION

VISION

Every day in every way I'm getting better, better and better! I am blessed and highly favored.

GRATITUDE

JOURNAL

On a scale of 1 - 10, How would you rate your effectiveness today? 1 2 3 4 5 6 7 8 9 10

DATE:

Write in complete sentences. i.e "Today I am...", "When I accomplish this..."

WILL

Declaration of intent for the day. What you will do.

OUTCOME

What you will feel when you accomplish this?

OBSTACLES

What could get in the way of you getting these things done?

PLAN & PRAY

What is the plan/how will you make sure it gets done? Then pray on it.

SEE

Imagine your day getting it all done and how it feels (60 seconds)

INTENSION

Who I want to BE today – e.g poised, aware, wise

INVOICE

Do you need to invoice the spirit for anything?

"Collaboration allows teachers to capture each other's fund of collective intelligence."
--Mike Schmoker

ATE:

POWER QUESTION

VISION

Every day in every way I'm getting better, better and better! I am blessed and highly favored.

GRATITUDE

JOURNAL

On a scale of 1 - 10, How would you rate your effectiveness today? 1 2 3 4 5 6 7 8 9 10

DATE:

Write in complete sentences. i.e "Today I am...", "When I accomplish this..."

WILL

Declaration of intent for the day. What you will do.

OUTCOME

What you will feel when you accomplish this?

OBSTACLES

What could get in the way of you getting these things done?

PLAN & PRAY

What is the plan/how will you make sure it gets done? Then pray on it.

SEE

Imagine your day getting it all done and how it feels (60 seconds)

INTENSION

Who I want to BE today – e.g poised, aware, wise

INVOICE

Do you need to invoice the spirit for anything?

"Health is a state of complete harmony of the body, mind and spirit. When one is free from physical disabilities and mental distractions, the gates of the soul open."
- B.K.S. Iyengar

ATE:

POWER QUESTION

VISION

Every day in every way I'm getting better, better and better! I am blessed and highly favored.

GRATITUDE

JOURNAL

On a scale of 1 - 10, How would you rate your effectiveness today? 1 2 3 4 5 6 7 8 9 10

DATE:

Write in complete sentences. i.e "Today I am...", "When I accomplish this..."

WILL

Declaration of intent for the day. What you will do.

OUTCOME

What you will feel when you accomplish this?

OBSTACLES

What could get in the way of you getting these things done?

PLAN & PRAY

What is the plan/how will you make sure it gets done? Then pray on it.

SEE

Imagine your day getting it all done and how it feels (60 seconds)

INTENSION

Who I want to BE today – e.g poised, aware, wise

INVOICE

Do you need to invoice the spirit for anything?

When health is absent, wisdom cannot reveal itself, art cannot become manifest, strength cannot be exerted, wealth is useless, and reason is powerless." - Herophiles

ATE:

POWER QUESTION

VISION

Every day in every way I'm getting better, better and better! I am blessed and highly favored.

GRATITUDE

JOURNAL

On a scale of 1 - 10, How would you rate your effectiveness today? 1 2 3 4 5 6 7 8 9 10

DATE:

Write in complete sentences. i.e "Today I am...", "When I accomplish this..."

WILL

Declaration of intent for the day. What you will do.

OUTCOME

What you will feel when you accomplish this?

OBSTACLES

What could get in the way of you getting these things done?

PLAN & PRAY

What is the plan/how will you make sure it gets done? Then pray on it.

SEE

Imagine your day getting it all done and how it feels (60 seconds)

INTENSION

Who I want to BE today – e.g poised, aware, wise

INVOICE

Do you need to invoice the spirit for anything?

"A man's health can be judged by which he takes two at a time–pills or stairs."
-Joan Welsh

ATE:

POWER QUESTION

VISION

Every day in every way I'm getting better, better and better! I am blessed and highly favored.

GRATITUDE

JOURNAL

On a scale of 1 - 10, How would you rate your effectiveness today? 1 2 3 4 5 6 7 8 9 10

DATE:

Write in complete sentences. i.e "Today I am...", "When I accomplish this..."

WILL

Declaration of intent for the day. What you will do.

OUTCOME

What you will feel when you accomplish this?

OBSTACLES

What could get in the way of you getting these things done?

PLAN & PRAY

What is the plan/how will you make sure it gets done? Then pray on it.

SEE

Imagine your day getting it all done and how it feels (60 seconds)

INTENSION

Who I want to BE today – e.g poised, aware, wise

INVOICE

Do you need to invoice the spirit for anything?

What drains your spirit, drains your body. What fuels your spirit, fuels your body." - Carolyn Myss

ATE:

POWER QUESTION

VISION

Every day in every way I'm getting better, better and better! I am blessed and highly favored.

GRATITUDE

JOURNAL

On a scale of 1 - 10, How would you rate your effectiveness today? 1 2 3 4 5 6 7 8 9 10

DATE:

Write in complete sentences. i.e "Today I am...", "When I accomplish this..."

WILL

Declaration of intent for the day. What you will do.

OUTCOME

What you will feel when you accomplish this?

OBSTACLES

What could get in the way of you getting these things done?

PLAN & PRAY

What is the plan/how will you make sure it gets done? Then pray on it.

SEE

Imagine your day getting it all done and how it feels (60 seconds)

INTENSION

Who I want to BE today – e.g poised, aware, wise

INVOICE

Do you need to invoice the spirit for anything?

"If you make listening and observation your occupation, you will gain much more than you can by talk." --Robert Baden-Powell

ATE:

POWER QUESTION

VISION

Every day in every way I'm getting better, better and better! I am blessed and highly favored.

GRATITUDE

JOURNAL

On a scale of 1 - 10, How would you rate your effectiveness today? 1 2 3 4 5 6 7 8 9 10

DATE:

Write in complete sentences. i.e "Today I am...", "When I accomplish this..."

WILL

Declaration of intent for the day. What you will do.

OUTCOME

What you will feel when you accomplish this?

OBSTACLES

What could get in the way of you getting these things done?

PLAN & PRAY

What is the plan/how will you make sure it gets done? Then pray on it.

SEE

Imagine your day getting it all done and how it feels (60 seconds)

INTENSION

Who I want to BE today – e.g poised, aware, wise

INVOICE

Do you need to invoice the spirit for anything?

"I just think we need more accountability and more transparency." --John Thune

ATE:

POWER QUESTION

VISION

Every day in every way I'm getting better, better and better! I am blessed and highly favored.

GRATITUDE

JOURNAL

On a scale of 1 - 10, How would you rate your effectiveness today? 1 2 3 4 5 6 7 8 9 10

DATE:

Write in complete sentences. i.e "Today I am...", "When I accomplish this..."

WILL

Declaration of intent for the day. What you will do.

OUTCOME

What you will feel when you accomplish this?

OBSTACLES

What could get in the way of you getting these things done?

PLAN & PRAY

What is the plan/how will you make sure it gets done? Then pray on it.

SEE

Imagine your day getting it all done and how it feels (60 seconds)

INTENSION

Who I want to BE today – e.g poised, aware, wise

INVOICE

Do you need to invoice the spirit for anything?

"If you haven't done much giving in your life-try it and see how you feel afterwards."
Michelle Moore, Selling Simplified

ATE:

POWER QUESTION

VISION

Every day in every way I'm getting better, better and better! I am blessed and highly favored.

GRATITUDE

JOURNAL

On a scale of 1 - 10, How would you rate your effectiveness today? 1 2 3 4 5 6 7 8 9 10

DATE:

Write in complete sentences. i.e "Today I am...", "When I accomplish this..."

WILL

Declaration of intent for the day. What you will do.

OUTCOME

What you will feel when you accomplish this?

OBSTACLES

What could get in the way of you getting these things done?

PLAN & PRAY

What is the plan/how will you make sure it gets done? Then pray on it.

SEE

Imagine your day getting it all done and how it feels (60 seconds)

INTENSION

Who I want to BE today – e.g poised, aware, wise

INVOICE

Do you need to invoice the spirit for anything?

"Those who tell the stories rule the world." --Hopi American Indian Proverb

ATE:

POWER QUESTION

VISION

Every day in every way I'm getting better, better and better! I am blessed and highly favored.

GRATITUDE

JOURNAL

On a scale of 1 - 10, How would you rate your effectiveness today? 1 2 3 4 5 6 7 8 9 10

DATE:

Write in complete sentences. i.e "Today I am...", "When I accomplish this..."

WILL

Declaration of intent for the day. What you will do.

OUTCOME

What you will feel when you accomplish this?

OBSTACLES

What could get in the way of you getting these things done?

PLAN & PRAY

What is the plan/how will you make sure it gets done? Then pray on it.

SEE

Imagine your day getting it all done and how it feels (60 seconds)

INTENSION

Who I want to BE today – e.g poised, aware, wise

INVOICE

Do you need to invoice the spirit for anything?

"The only disease you have is your inability to see you have the power to heal yourself." - Ralph Smart

ATE:

POWER QUESTION

VISION

Every day in every way I'm getting better, better and better! I am blessed and highly favored.

GRATITUDE

JOURNAL

On a scale of 1 - 10, How would you rate your effectiveness today? 1 2 3 4 5 6 7 8 9 10

DATE:

Write in complete sentences. i.e "Today I am...", "When I accomplish this..."

WILL

Declaration of intent for the day. What you will do.

OUTCOME

What you will feel when you accomplish this?

OBSTACLES

What could get in the way of you getting these things done?

PLAN & PRAY

What is the plan/how will you make sure it gets done? Then pray on it.

SEE

Imagine your day getting it all done and how it feels (60 seconds)

INTENSION

Who I want to BE today – e.g poised, aware, wise

INVOICE

Do you need to invoice the spirit for anything?

"Divide each difficulty into as many parts as is feasible and necessary to resolve it, and watch the whole transform." - Rene Descartes

ATE:

POWER QUESTION

VISION

Every day in every way I'm getting better, better and better! I am blessed and highly favored.

GRATITUDE

JOURNAL

On a scale of 1 - 10, How would you rate your effectiveness today? 1 2 3 4 5 6 7 8 9 10

Time for your 90 day check-in P.T.O

DATE:

CONGRATULATIONS! YOU DID IT!!

Revisiting My Why

Use this section to contemplate why you set these goals 30 days ago and how important that still is for you.

Expectations

Review where you expected to be by this point. Are you ahead, on track, behind? Evaluate those results and determine whether ot not you may need to pivot.

Effectiveness

Use this section to evaluate you're effectiveness. What is working? What isn't working? How can you do more of what's working and change what is not working?

Next Steps

Write out clearly what your goals are moving forward and where you aspire to be in the next 90 days. How will you celebrate your accomplishments? Make a plan to celebrate yourself and implement it.

WOOPSII Journal

Accountability Partner Section

•

Accountability Success Framework

Tasha Danvers

Email **woopsiijournal@gmail.com** for more information on connecting with an Accountability Partner

DATE: 23rd June, This Year

Accountability Success Framework

EXAMPLE

Accountability Partner

Destiny Angel

Accountability Partner's (HTG) Hot Ticket Goal

Start a Sunday spiritual group for women.

WINS /PROGRESS

Asked 5 friends to ask at least 3 of their friends, if they would be interested in joining the group. Set the monthly membership rate and drew up a 12 week curriculum.

SETBACKS / CHALLENGES

Struggling to find a website and branding person that does what I want and is within my budget.

CORRECTIONS / FIXES

Meditate + pray on finding the right person that God has assigned to do this job. Ask God who my Destiny Angels are to support me on this. Speak to people I know who have businesses etc that may have intel.

SUPPORT NEEDED

More people to get the word out. Someone who can support with social media.

KEY LEARNING

Learned a lot about website building and what I will need to get the job done. Also got a good idea of what the price point is for the type of website I want. Also found there may be funding for me through SBC

ACTION STEPS & BY WHEN

Ask Janet + Devon if they know anyone for branding. See if Kiana can help with getting started on social media.

ATE:

Accountability Success Framework

Accountability Partner

Accountability Partner's (HTG) Hot Ticket Goal

WINS /PROGRESS

SETBACKS / CHALLENGES

CORRECTIONS / FIXES

SUPPORT NEEDED

KEY LEARNING

ACTION STEPS & BY WHEN

DATE:

Accountability Success Framework

Accountability Partner

Accountability Partner's (HTG) Hot Ticket Goal

WINS /PROGRESS

SETBACKS / CHALLENGES

CORRECTIONS / FIXES

SUPPORT NEEDED

KEY LEARNING

ACTION STEPS & BY WHEN

ATE:

Accountability Success Framework

Accountability Partner

Accountability Partner's (HTG) Hot Ticket Goal

WINS /PROGRESS

SETBACKS / CHALLENGES

CORRECTIONS / FIXES

SUPPORT NEEDED

KEY LEARNING

ACTION STEPS & BY WHEN

DATE:

Accountability Success Framework

Accountability Partner

Accountability Partner's (HTG) Hot Ticket Goal

WINS /PROGRESS

SETBACKS / CHALLENGES

CORRECTIONS / FIXES

SUPPORT NEEDED

KEY LEARNING

ACTION STEPS & BY WHEN

ATE:

Accountability Success Framework

Accountability Partner

Accountability Partner's (HTG) Hot Ticket Goal

WINS /PROGRESS

SETBACKS / CHALLENGES

CORRECTIONS / FIXES

SUPPORT NEEDED

KEY LEARNING

ACTION STEPS & BY WHEN

DATE:

Accountability Success Framework

Accountability Partner

Accountability Partner's (HTG) Hot Ticket Goal

WINS /PROGRESS

SETBACKS / CHALLENGES

CORRECTIONS / FIXES

SUPPORT NEEDED

KEY LEARNING

ACTION STEPS & BY WHEN

ATE:

Accountability Success Framework

Accountability Partner

Accountability Partner's (HTG) Hot Ticket Goal

WINS /PROGRESS

SETBACKS / CHALLENGES

CORRECTIONS / FIXES

SUPPORT NEEDED

KEY LEARNING

ACTION STEPS & BY WHEN

DATE:

Accountability Success Framework

Accountability Partner

Accountability Partner's (HTG) Hot Ticket Goal

WINS /PROGRESS

SETBACKS / CHALLENGES

CORRECTIONS / FIXES

SUPPORT NEEDED

KEY LEARNING

ACTION STEPS & BY WHEN

ATE:

Accountability Success Framework

Accountability Partner

Accountability Partner's (HTG) Hot Ticket Goal

WINS /PROGRESS

SETBACKS / CHALLENGES

CORRECTIONS / FIXES

SUPPORT NEEDED

KEY LEARNING

ACTION STEPS & BY WHEN

DATE:

Accountability Success Framework

Accountability Partner

Accountability Partner's (HTG) Hot Ticket Goal

WINS /PROGRESS

SETBACKS / CHALLENGES

CORRECTIONS / FIXES

SUPPORT NEEDED

KEY LEARNING

ACTION STEPS & BY WHEN

ATE:

Accountability Success Framework

Accountability Partner

Accountability Partner's (HTG) Hot Ticket Goal

WINS /PROGRESS

SETBACKS / CHALLENGES

CORRECTIONS / FIXES

SUPPORT NEEDED

KEY LEARNING

ACTION STEPS & BY WHEN

DATE:

Accountability Success Framework

Accountability Partner

Accountability Partner's (HTG) Hot Ticket Goal

WINS /PROGRESS

SETBACKS / CHALLENGES

CORRECTIONS / FIXES

SUPPORT NEEDED

KEY LEARNING

ACTION STEPS & BY WHEN

ATE:

Accountability Success Framework

Accountability Partner

Accountability Partner's (HTG) Hot Ticket Goal

WINS /PROGRESS

SETBACKS / CHALLENGES

CORRECTIONS / FIXES

SUPPORT NEEDED

KEY LEARNING

ACTION STEPS & BY WHEN

DATE:

Accountability Success Framework

Accountability Partner

Accountability Partner's (HTG) Hot Ticket Goal

WINS /PROGRESS

SETBACKS / CHALLENGES

CORRECTIONS / FIXES

SUPPORT NEEDED

KEY LEARNING

ACTION STEPS & BY WHEN

NOTES

NOTES

NOTES

NOTES

NOTES

NOTES

NOTES

NOTES

ather in Job 22:28 you said 'I shall decree a thing, and it shall be tablished unto me, and the light shall shine upon my ways'. I decree all ese things. Let it be so.

- I decree and declare I am experiencing God's faithfulness. I am keeping my trust in him knowing that He will not fail me. I am giving birth to every promise that God put in my heart and I am daily stepping into everything He created me to be.
- I decree and declare God's incredible blessings over my life. I am seeing an explosion of God's goodness and a sudden widespread of increase. I am experiencing the surpassing greatness of God's favor. Through His favor I am elevated to a level higher than I ever dreamed of. I am experiencing explosive blessings.
- I decree and declare I have the grace I need for today. I am full of power, strength, and determination. Nothing I face is too much for me. I am overcoming every obstacle, outlasting every challenge, and coming through every difficulty.
- I decree and declare now is the time to accomplish everything God has placed in my heart. My window of opportunity is now. God has moments of favor in my present and future. He is preparing me right now, because He is constantly releasing a special grace to help me accomplish those dreams. This is my time, this is my moment. I receive and allow it today.
- I decree and declare I am grateful for who God is in my life and for what He's done. I am not taking for granted the people, the opportunities, and the favor He has blessed me with. I am looking at what is right and not what is wrong. I am thanking Him for what I have, and not complaining about what I don't have. I am seeing each day as a gift from God. My heart is overflowing with praise and gratitude for all His goodness.
- I decree and declare a legacy of faith over my life.
- I decree and declare that I am storing up blessings for future generations. My life is marked by excellence and integrity. Because I'm making right choices and taking steps of faith, others want to follow me. God's abundance is surrounding my life today.

Daily Decree & Declaration

- I decree and declare that God has a great plan for my life. He is directing my steps. And even though I may not always understand how, I know my situation is not a surprise to God. He will work out every detail to my advantage in His perfect timing, everything will turn out right.
- I decree and declare God's dream for my life is coming to pass. It will not be stopped by people, disappointments, or adversities. God has solutions to every problem I will ever face already lined up. The right people and the right breaks are coming now. I am fulfilling my destiny.
- I decree and declare a multitude of blessings are coming my way. I am progressive, productive, and abundant. God pours me out a blessing so abundant I do not have room enough to receive it.
- I decree and declare my capacity for love, creativity, and self mastery a ever expanding. God is opening up supernatural doors for me. He is speaking to the right people about me. I am seeing Ephesians 3:20, exceedingly, abundantly, above and beyond favor and increase in my lif Because I honor him, His blessings chase me down and overtake me. I ar in the right place at the right time. People go out of their way to be gooc to me. I am surrounded by God's favor.
- I decree and declare I am special and extraordinary. I am not average. I have been custom-made. I am one of a kind. Of all the things God created, what He is most proud of is me. I am His Masterpiece, His most prized possession. I am keeping my head held high, knowing I am a child of the most high God made in His very image.
- I decree and declare that I am using my words to bless people. I am speaking favor and victory over my family, friends, and loved ones. I am helping call out their seeds of greatness by telling them “I'm proud of you, I love you, you are amazing, you are talented, you are beautiful, yol are doing great things in this life.
- I decree and declare that I have a sound mind filled with good thoughts, use my authority to crush any thoughts of defeat or failure. By faith, I ar well able. I am anointed. I am equipped. I am empowered. My thoughts are guided by God's Word everyday. No obstacle can defeat me becaus my mind is programmed for victory.

- I decree and declare that I live as a healer. I am sensitive to the needs of those around me. I lift the fallen, restore the broken, and encourage the discouraged. I am full of compassion and kindness. I won't just look for a miracle. I am becoming someone's miracle by showing God's love and mercy everywhere I go.
- I decree and declare I put actions behind my faith. I am bold and conscientious. I demonstrate my faith by taking bold steps to move towards what God has put in my heart. My faith is not hidden. It is seen. I know when God sees my faith He is showing up and doing amazing things.
- I decree and declare breakthroughs are happening in my life. Sudden bursts of God's goodness. Not a trickle. Not a stream, but a flood of God's power. A flood of healing. A flood of wisdom. A flood of favor. I am a breakthrough person and I choose to live breakthrough-minded. I am expecting God to overwhelm me with His goodness and amaze me with His favor.
- I decree and declare that I am calm and peaceful. I glide through challenging situations. I rise above every difficulty knowing that God has given me the power to remain calm. I choose to live my life happy, bloom where I am planted, and let God fight my battles.
- I decree and declare God's supernatural favor over my life. What I cannot make happen on my own, God makes happen for me. Supernatural opportunities, supernatural healing, supernatural restoration, and supernatural breakthroughs are happening now. I am getting stronger, healthier, and wiser. I am discovering talents that I did not know I had, and I am accomplishing my God given dream.
- I decree and declare I am a people builder. I look for opportunities to encourage others, to break out the best in them, and to help them accomplish their dreams. I am speaking words of faith and victory, affirming them, approving them, letting them know they are valued. I am calling out seeds of greatness, helping them to rise higher and be all that God created them to be.

Daily Decree & Declaration

- I decree and declare I am speaking only positive words of faith and victory over myself, my life partner, my family, and my future. I am usin my words to specifically change my situation. I am calling in favor, good breaks, healing, and restoration. I am not talking to God about how big my problems are, I am talking to my problems about how big my God is.
- I decree and declare that I thrive. I prosper despite every difficulty that may come my way. I know every setback is a setup for a comeback. I am always increasing, I go after my dreams, and I always strive to grow. I know one touch of God's favor changes everything. I am ready for a yea of blessings and a year of thriving.
- I decree and declare I am choosing faith over fear. I meditate on what is positive and what is good about my situation. I am using my energy to believe. Faith is at the core of my being. I dwell on positive encouraging thoughts. My mind is set on what God says about me. I know His plan fo me is success, victory and abundance.
- I decree and declare I am equipped for every good work God has planne for me. I am anointed and empowered by the creator of the universe. Every bondage, every limitation is broken off of me now. This is my time to shine. I am rising higher, overcoming every obstacle, and experiencin victory like never before.
- I decree and declare that I confidently ask God for big things in my life. I am praying bold prayers, and I expect big and believe big. I am asking God to bring to pass those hidden dreams that are deep in my heart. If certain promises don't look like they are happening, I continue to trust and keep my faith in God. I am praying with boldness, expecting God to show himself strong, knowing that nothing is too difficult for Him.
- I decree and declare that God is working all things together for my good. He has a master plan for my life. There may be things I don't understand right now, but I am faithful and at peace. I know all the pieces aren't here yet. One day it will all come together and everything will make sense. I ar seeing God's amazing plan taking me places I never dreamed of.

Daily Decree & Declaration

- I decree and declare everything that doesn't line up with God's vision for my life is subject to change. Any challenges are temporary because my life is always a reflection of health, wealth, love, and perfect self expression. I am moved by what I know, by the spiritual realm and nothing else. I am a victor. I am a warrior. I am becoming all God has created me to be.
- I decree and declare that I walk in the blessings of the almighty God. I am filled with wisdom. I make good choices. I have clear direction.
- I decree and declare I am blessed with creativity, with good ideas, with courage, with strength, and with ability.
- I decree and declare I am blessed with good health, a good family, good friends, and a long life.
- I decree and declare I am blessed with promotion, with success, with an obedient heart, and with a positive outlook.
- I decree and declare whatever I put my hands to is prospering and succeeding. I am blessed in the city and blessed in the field. I am blessed when I go in and blessed when I go out.
- I decree and declare I lend and not borrow and I am above and not beneath.
- I decree and declare right now that every negative word, every curse that has ever been spoken over me is broken in the name of Jesus.
- I decree and declare the negative things that have been in my family even for generations no longer have any effect on me.
- I decree and declare that from this day forward I am experiencing a new sense of freedom, a new happiness, and a new fulfillment.
- I decree and declare that I am blessed. I believe in the spiritual realm things have already been set into motion. Curses have been broken, and blessings are active in my life right now. The Bible says when you align your thoughts with God's thoughts and you start dwelling on the promises of His Word, when you constantly dwell on thoughts of His victory, favor, faith, power, and strength, nothing can hold you back. Deuteronomy 31:1

1 Thessalonians 5:18

Heavenly Father, I thank you that this is already done,
I know it, I believe it, and I allow it!

Mark 11:22-24

Originally created by @George4JC
Updated, revised & reworded by Tasha Danvers @TashaTheOlympian

Made in the USA
Columbia, SC
19 August 2024